Prelude

"If you have to ask what Jazz is, you will never know"
Louis Armstrong

For a long time, I had wanted to capture my memories of listening to Jazz over a lifetime as a Jazz fan, before the memories faded. Retiring from Lecturing gave me that opportunity.

When I started writing, my objective was simply to talk about recordings I had enjoyed and to include reminiscences of Jazz events.

Before I was a month into the project, researching the people behind the music, I realized that the scope had become wider. I found myself discovering musicians whose music I had not enjoyed and others to whom I had not listened.

I would also add that much of my Jazz listening was done while I was driving my car. Being able to see on video, Jazz performances I had only heard before, has added a whole new dimension to my enjoyment.

Thus, as I have been writing, I have been listening to and watching a lot of recent music, as well as many of my old favourites.

This may also be the time to mention that I have no musical talent whatsoever, I just enjoy listening. Looking back at the music I have enjoyed; I realize there had to be a "hook" to catch me. It may be melody, rhythm, or the beat. I recognize now how much this limitation has influenced the Jazz I enjoy most. That is not an apology, it is a statement of fact.

I totally share the views of Ross Porter, long-time President of Jazz FM 91 in Toronto. He said *"I crave music that grabs my attention. It gives me a feeling of wonder, appreciation, and it makes me feel good.*[1]

I have explored Jazz from two major perspectives; a chronology of Jazz from the time I started to listen to it in the 1950s and a section on musicians and vocalists I have enjoyed over the years. I added a section on Jazz in Canada, where I have lived since 1985.

As I have explored ideas during this exercise, I have frequently come across the notion that Jazz is dead, or at least dying. It has certainly lost a large part of its following, but it has changed, and must change more. I will talk a little about this in the Finale of my opus, and for my next project I want to write about the musicians who hold the future of Jazz in their hands.

I have learned so much and discovered so much new music over the past few months, and have greatly enjoyed the research, the listening, the viewing, and the writing. I hope I have created something you will enjoy reading.

Tony Carter

Table of Contents

Part One. A Jazz Chronology

My Early Years of Jazz

"Jazz of the sort we play is a happy, extroverted music. You don't have to think about it too much "

. Chris Barber [2]

I bought my very first Jazz record in about 1956. It was "Muskrat Ramble" by **Ted "Kid" Ory** [1886 – 1973].

Edward "Kid" Ory was the most important influence on other Jazz trombonists.

He started on the banjo when he was ten, soon switching to valve trombone and eventually permanently to slide trombone.

His playing impressed Buddy Bolden so much that Bolden offered him a job. But due to family obligations, Ory had to reluctantly turn him down. Ory did move to New Orleans in 1910. He became one of the most important bandleaders in the city. Joe "King" Oliver was his cornetist for a time. Clarinetist Sidney Bechet, was also a member of the band.

When he made the decision to move to Chicago, Ory had two jobs waiting for him playing nightly with King Oliver and recording with Louis Armstrong's Hot Five.

He also had the chance to make the recording debut of his most famous original "Muskrat Ramble" on February 26, 1926

I have no idea where I first heard Muskrat Ramble, but it was to influence my Jazz listening for at least the next five years.

England in the 1950s was the home of "Traditional" Jazz. Traditional Jazz was essentially derived from "Dixieland" Jazz. It was not until later that I discovered some of the amazing Jazz music that was being played in the USA. We traditionalists, somewhat scornfully, labeled it "Modern Jazz."

1

The biggest name in British Jazz at that time was **Humphrey Lyttleton** [1921 – 2008]. Humphrey Lyttleton excelled at everything that he chose to do. He was a trumpeter, bandleader, calligrapher, cartoonist, writer, journalist, and broadcaster.

He also had the doubtful distinction of having descended from another Humphrey Lytttleton, who was hanged for his part in the Gunpowder Plot of 1605.

Lyttleton played the trumpet, as did most bandleaders of the time, and had much in common with his clarinet player, Wally Fawkes, who was also known as "Flook" a cartoonist for the Daily Mail.

He had a very wide audience and in 1956 his composition "Bad Penny Blues" became a Top Twenty hit. He had achieved a balance between "popular" and "traditional."

Humphrey Lyttleton made a recording in 2003 with singer Elkie Brooks, whom he had first worked with in 1963. The CD is called "Trouble in Mind." Most of the tracks are slow bluesy numbers and Humph's trumpet playing is just so melodious. It brought back so many memories, and I still enjoy "Bad Penny Blues" from over half a century ago.

The number two Jazz band at the time was Chris Barber's. Chris Barber [1930 - 2021] originally partnered with Ken Colyer, but they broke up in 1954 and Colyer formed his own band. Chris Barber played the trombone. His trumpet player was Pat Halcox who joined the band when Ken Colyer left in 1954 and played with Chris Barber until he retired, 54 years later.

Barber enjoyed many genres of music, but he never relinquished the conviction that Jazz was his era's freshest and most resourceful music and that the more the world knew of it, the better.

The Chris Barber Band of the 1950s was the starting point of some famous careers. One of them was an amazing young Irish girl, called Ottilie Patterson. She was a Blues Singer, and fellow blues enthusiast, the vocalist George Melly, likened her to Bessie Smith. **Ottilie Patterson** 1932 – 2011] herself said. *"I sing the blues because I find it so fulfilling,"* [3]and it showed.

2

The next graduate of the band was **Lonnie Donegan** [1931 - 2002]. Most Traditional Jazz Bands at the time had a banjo player. Donegan was Chris Barber's banjo player but was best known for reviving skiffle music, which had originated in the extremely poor parts of the Deep South of the USA in the 1920s.

There is an amusing story, when Chris Barber reputedly said that he made more money on royalties from Lonnie's "Rock Island Line" than from his own trombone playing.

The instruments included washboard, jugs, tea chest bass, kazoo, cigar box fiddle, comb and paper, guitar, and banjo. Is skiffle jazz music? That is debatable, but its popularity for the second half of the 1950s was undeniable.

The third name to mention is **Monty Sunshine** [1928 – 2010]; Chris Barber's clarinetist. He soloed on one of the best-selling jazz recordings of the time; "Petite Fleur."

Chris Barber himself retired in 2019 at the age of eighty-nine.

The clarinet as a jazz instrument was probably at the height of its popularity, and it is worth mentioning **Acker Bilk** [1929 – 2014]. Acker Bilk was one of the characters of English Jazz at the time with his distinctive appearance – of a goatee, bowler hat and striped waistcoat, together with a broad West Country accent.

It is almost a pity that his greatest hit "Stranger by the Shore," a very commercial offering, outshone a lot of first-rate good jazz music.

Other popular Traditional Jazz Bands were led by **Ken Colyer** [1928 – 1988], **Kenny Ball** [1930 – 2013], and **Mick Mulligan** [1928 – 2006].

Mick Mulligan's was not the best band, but they were fun to watch. When I was at University in Reading, we had a particularly good Jazz Club, and we attracted some of the top names. Mick Mulligan was always popular, and the highlight of the evening was when Pete Appleby played a 20-minute drum solo of the Jazz Classic, "Christopher Columbus, while the rest of the band adjourned to the bar to enjoy a quick 3 or 4 pints of beer.

Chris Barber's quote about extroverts certainly applies to the next two bands I want to talk about.

The Temperance Seven was founded in 1955 by students at the Chelsea School of Art, though the band created the myth that its creation dated from 1904 at the fictitious Pasadena Cocoa Rooms, Balls Pond Road, London. The band evolved into a nine-piece ensemble with a light-hearted and humorous performing style, although they were all serious musicians.

Cephas Howard led the band ["Captain Cashiered"] who played the trumpet and euphonium. The band constantly reflected the so-called "authenticity" of their early days by using instruments like the euphonium, the sousaphone, and the tuba, rather than the upright bass.

The vocalist with the band was "Whispering" Paul McDowell [1931 – 2016]. McDowell was a college friend of most of the Temperance Seven. His main career interest lay in acting, but he reluctantly joined the band. "McDowell's deadpan delivery of the lyrics was crucial to the success of You're Driving Me Crazy, which was followed in quick succession by three more hit singles in 1961, of which " Pasadena" was the biggest seller.

McDowell quickly became bored and after his brief period as an unwilling pop star this *"chaotic genius"*, as the filmmaker Julian Doyle called him, had a varied career as a scriptwriter, actor, painter and tai chi teacher.

After his departure, The Temperance Seven never achieved the same success.

Traditional Jazz at this time was very much a British phenomenon, but an interesting band emerged in the USA.

The Firehouse Five Plus Two called themselves "America's Favorite Jazz Band" and were considered a national institution. Their colorful firefighters' uniforms complete with genuine antique leather fire hats, and their 1914 American La France firetruck were familiar sights to millions.

All this is the more remarkable for having been part-time musicians. The band was led by Ward Kimball: trombone, siren, tambourine, sound effects, who was a lead animator and director for Disney studios. All members of the band were employed by Disney Studios.

The band was formed in 1951, and over the next 20 years was enormously popular, particularly on TV.

The great age of Traditional Jazz in England ended in the early 1960s when music became dominated by the Beatles and the Merseyside sound. As I was living in Liverpool at the time, I followed the crowd and deserted Jazz for a while.

1950s Golden Age of Jazz

"Jazz speaks for life. This is triumphant music"
Martin Luther King, Jr.

"The 1950s were a time of changes and the music of the decade both reflected the cultural changes that were happening'. Following the detrimental effects of World War II, the United States was about to embark on a musical journey that would change the face of music for decades to come. "[4]

Looking back at the 1950s I wonder if people realized how important that period was in terms of the development of music. Those were my teenage years, and my love of traditional Jazz was challenged by the new wave of popular music.

Rock 'n' Roll Musicians included: Elvis Presley, Jerry Lee Lewis, Little Richard, Chubby Checker, Billy Haley and Buddy Holly.

Pop Musicians included: Nat King Cole, Rosemary Clooney, Perry Como, Dean Martin, Tony Bennett, Peggy Lee, Johnny Mathis, Andy Williams, Frank Sinatra, and Frankie Laine. There was some crossover at this time, and several of these made jazz recordings.

Jazz Music also showed many changes in the 1950s, although I was not aware of it all at the time, partly because of my enthusiasm for rock n' roll, and partly because the UK banned US artists from coming to Britain.

The 1940s jazz scene had been dominated by Big Band Jazz and Swing and Big Band carried over to the 1950s. My interest started with the Glenn Miller Story [1953] and was reinforced by The Benny Goodman Story [1956].

The greatest Big Band Leaders must be **Duke Ellington** [1899 – 1974] and **Count Basie** [1904 – 1984]. By the 1950s they were both well established and continued to be a major force in the 1950s, and I still enjoy listening to their music today.

Duke Ellington was an enormously popular pianist, composer, and big-band leader. He and Count Basie were the most important bandleaders in jazz history. Although known for his pioneering in Jazz,

Ellington also excelled in various other genres, including gospel, blues, classical, and pop. We also need to remember he was a brilliant pianist. Because of his charisma and inventive use of his orchestra, Ellington is responsible for making Jazz an art form, akin to classical music.

A considerable number of musicians have been inspired by the "Duke," including Thelonius Monk, Sonny Stitt, Tony Bennett, Dizzy Gillespie, Oscar Peterson, Earl Hines, Charles Mingus. and Joe Pass.

My favourite Duke Ellington tune "Take the A Train." was written in 1939 by **Billy Strayhorn** [1915 – 1967], and first recorded in 1941. Strayhorn was a pianist, composer and arranger who worked with Ellington for over 30 years. The story behind A Train is one of the legends of jazz history. "Take the 'A' Train" was composed, after Ellington offered Strayhorn a job in his organization and gave him money to travel from Pittsburgh to Harlem, Ellington wrote directions for Strayhorn to get to his house by subway, directions that began, "Take the A Train".

Groundbreaking pianist, organist, composer, and bandleader Count Basie led one of the most successful bands in history. For 50 years, the Count Basie Orchestra, an incredibly popular group of musicians including Lester Young, Harry "Sweets" Edison, Buck Clayton, and Joe Williams, maintained one of the most swinging and hard- hitting bands in America.

Basie introduced multiple generations of listeners to the big band sound. He created numerous standards like "April in Paris" and "One O'clock Jump," which have been covered by countless other artists.

It is great fun to listen to other versions, my favourite is still the Count Basie 1955 recording. On this recording, trumpeter Thad Jones played his famous "Pop Goes the Weasel" solo, and Basie directed the band to play the chorus "one more time" and then "one more once." One of Jazz's magic moments

His colleagues also remember Basie as being considerate, modest, relaxed, and enthusiastic. Without Basie's presence on the stage, popular and big band music would be drastically different and undoubtedly less influential than it has become.

Both Basie and Ellington had careers going back to the 1930s, but to me they were a focal point of the 1950s "The Golden Age of Jazz."

First Time! The Count Meets the Duke[5] is an album by Basie and Ellington with their combined Orchestras.

Big Bands continued to be successful, and I also enjoyed listening to Stan Kenton and Woody Herman.

Stan Kenton [1911-1979] had a career lasting four decades, matching that of Count Basie, Duke Ellington, and Woody Herman. Like Basie and Ellington, Kenton was a pianist. His style varied over the years, but he always came back to the Big Band style. One of his biggest failures was to experiment with a 39-piece orchestra including a large string section.

When I first heard Stan Kenton, which would have been in the 1960s, I heard an enormous difference to other big bands of the time. Michael Boyd in a 1987 article described it like this *'Kenton's sound was more aggressive and even occasionally more abrasive than of other bands. The saxophones played strongly, with screaming trumpets, and a lush, rich trombone sound.'*[6] A word I would use is "driving." Kenton was at his peak in the 1950s and included many well-known names: Maynard Ferguson, Shorty Rogers, Art Pepper, Shelly Manne, and vocalist June Christy.

He was not universally popular, partly because of a reverse racial prejudice, claiming that as a white musician, he was unfairly treated.

Like the influence Billy Strayhorn had on the Duke Ellington band, many of Kenton's most successful recordings were composed and arranged by **Pete Rugolo** [1915 – 2011]. Rugolo was born in Sicily, but came to the USA as a child, and quickly followed in his father's musical footsteps. He received a bachelor's degree and then went on to study composition with Darius Milhaud and earn his master's degree.[7] Another famous student of Milhaud was Dave Brubeck.

Stan Kenton is probably best known for his version of "Peanut Vendor," but I also like a very contrasting piece "Artistry in Rhythm."

Woody Herman [1913 – 1987] is the fourth of my favourite Big Band Leaders. Like Benny Goodman, Herman was a clarinetist, and both were giants of the swing era. When I was reading more about him, I was surprised to learn that his greatest hit "At the Woodchoppers' Ball" was recorded as early as 1939. His tune "Apple Honey," which drew its origin from George Gershwin's "I got Rhythm" was clearly his favourite and appears on almost all his albums.

There is a great 1944 recording on YouTube[8], in which Woody himself plays a leading role. The video is worth watching because the photos and posters create an interesting picture of Woody Herman's career.

Like Stan Kenton several musicians got their start with Woody Herman, including saxophonists Zoot Sims and Stan Getz, and drummer Shelley Manne.

Other successful bandleaders in the 1950s included Arty Shaw, Jack Teagarden, Ray Anthony, Tommy and Jimmy Dorsey, Les Brown and Billy Eckstine, who went on to enjoy a successful career as a vocalist.

But by the end of the '50s economics were forcing the Big Bands out of the limelight, because 15-piece bands were too expensive to continue.

I had not originally included **Benny Goodman** [1909 – 1986] in my list, although I enjoyed his music. I found that his contribution to jazz history was much greater than the Swing Band, and I have listened to much of his small group music.

Adding **Lionel Hampton** on vibraphone was an inspired move and I particularly enjoy "Flying Home"[9] which also features Charlie Christian. This was recorded in 1939.

Innovation in the 1950s

The 1950s was also a period of innovation. To me the most exciting new sound came from the Modern Jazz Quartet. The original members of the group: **John Lewis** [1920 – 2001], **Milt Jackson** [1923 – 1999], **Ray Brown** [1926 – 2002], and **Kenny Clarke** [1914 – 1985] were the rhythm section of Dizzy Gillespie's band. Gillespie himself encouraged them to play sets on their own at his concerts.

Ray Brown left early on to focus on working with his wife, Ella Fitzgerald and was replaced by **Percy Heath** [1923 – 2005]. Clarke left after about three years saying, *"I wouldn't be able to play the drums my way again after four or five years of playing eighteenth-century drawing-room Jazz[10]"*. His replacement, **Connie Kay** [1927 – 1984], proved to be the perfect fit for the way MJQ was evolving.

There is so much wonderful music recorded by MJQ, with most of it being composed by John Lewis. My favourite album is "Django," which includes a tribute to Django Reinhardt, who had died in 1954, a year before this recording. Miles Davis described "Django" as one of the finest pieces of jazz music ever written. The album also features "Queen's Fancy" and "Delauney's Dilemma," two of my favourite MJQ recordings.

Although from a later period [1973], a favourite album of mine is "Blues to Bach", especially "Precious Joy". This adaptation can also be recognized as "Jesu, Joy of Man's Desiring" On this album, John Lewis shows his versatility and captures the mood perfectly by playing harpsichord as well as piano. I probably still listen to the timeless music of MJQ more than anything else in my collection.

One of the thoughts that goes through my mind when I listen to **Dave Brubeck** [1920-2012] is that he was trained in classical music and that influenced his style of music, experimenting with time signatures throughout his career. The effect captivated me.

Brubeck played on the West coast during the 1950s, already having **Paul Desmond** [1924-1977] as a partner. They met while in the military in 1944, and Desmond worked with Brubeck until his death from lung cancer.

But it was not until 1959 that the "Time Out" album, which included "Take Five" was released. Almost all the tracks used an unconventional time signature and initially Brubeck was unwilling to release it as he considered it to be experimental, being based largely on Eurasian music he had heard on tour. It became a platinum seller.

One of my favourite pieces "Blue Rondo a la Turk" is also featured on the album. Another of my favourites "It's a Raggy Waltz" is on the follow-up album "Further Time Out."

In 1958 African American bassist **Eugene Wright** [1923-2020] joined for the group's U.S. Department of State tour of Europe and Asia the group visited Poland, Türkiye, India, Sri Lanka (then Ceylon), Pakistan, Iran and Iraq on behalf of the U.S. Government.[11]

"During the late 1950s and early 1960s Brubeck cancelled several concerts because the club owners or hall managers continued to resist the idea of an integrated band on their stages. He also cancelled a television appearance when he found out that the producers intended to keep Wright off-camera." [12]

This was the beginning of a period of racial tension, and Jazz was caught up in it. I admire Brubeck's stance on this.

I have not come close to doing justice to the 1950s in Jazz, so let me end this chapter by talking about an event which comes close to capturing the essence of the period.

A Great Day in Harlem

A Great Day in Harlem is a black-and-white photograph of 57 Jazz musicians in Harlem, New York City. The picture was taken by photographer Art Kane for Esquire magazine on August 12, 1958. *Esquire* published the photo in its January 1959 issue.

There is a delightful quote from Dizzy Gillespie, who said: " *When I found out there was to be this big meeting, I said to myself This is my chance to see all these great musicians without having to go to a funeral*" [13]

Art Kane, who took the picture tells the story of one of the night-owl musicians, sadly nameless, who said that "*he was astonished that there were two ten o'clocks in the day*" [14]

Count Basie got bored and in the final picture, he is sitting on the kerb with a crowd of neighbourhood kids who had gathered to enjoy the fun.

The musicians in the photograph included: Count Basie, Art Blakey, Buck Clayton, Miles Davis, Vic Dickenson, Roy Eldridge, Art Farmer, Dizzy Gillespie, Benny Golson, Coleman Hawkins, Hank Jones, Gene Krupa, Marian McPartland, Charles Mingus, Thelonious Monk, Gerry Mulligan, Sonny Rollins, Horace Silver, Mary Lou Williams and Lester Young.

Saxophonists Benny Golson [Born 1929], and Sonny Rollins [Born 1920] are the only living members of the fifty-seven people who were in the picture.

Memories of that day are fondly held. Jean Bach, a radio producer of New York, recounted the story behind the photograph in her 1994 documentary film, *A Great Day in Harlem*. This incorporated 8 mm film footage taken by bassist Milt Hinton on the day.

In 2018, a book was published to mark the 60th anniversary of the event, with forewords by Quincy Jones and Benny Golson and an introduction by Kane's son, Jonathan. .

Especially for those of us who were familiar with the 1957 event will have enjoyed the 2004 movie "The Terminal". Tom Hanks, an East European tourist, was on a mission to get the final autograph of the only musician, whose autograph he did not have, that of Benny Golson. It is a delightful subplot to a very funny movie, and a small cameo role for Benny Golson topped it off beautifully.

Norman Granz: The Great Influencer

There will never be another decade like the 1950s for Jazz. "Norman Granz [1918 – 2001] was arguably the most important non-musician in Jazz" Norman Granz was a record producer, a concert producer and manager of great musicians.

He started his involvement on the jazz scene in the 1940s when he opened a club in Los Angeles where he invited musicians, simply to "jam". This evolved in the 1950s into what I think was one of the greatest innovations for jazz fans. Jazz at the Philharmonic also started in LA, but toured the country, enabling jazz fans outside the major cities like New York and Chicago.

A typical session consisted of 8 or 9 musicians from an amazing collection of names, including: Oscar Peterson, Barney Kessel, Stan Getz, Charlie Parker, Ray Brown, Harry Edison, Buddy Rich, and Lionel Hampton. They were jam sessions, and there are nine JATP recordings. These are available on 5 CD's and as Ross Porter says, *"this a great opportunity to hear Jazz history in the making"*.[15]

As a promoter, Granz was fearless, and would accept no racial obstacles, going as far as cancelling a sold-out concert when he learned the audience was to be segregated. All JATP groups were a mix of Black and white musicians. Jazz at the Philharmonic ended as the 1950s ended, and Granz chose to move to Switzerland.

I did not know until recently that Norman Granz made two movies. The first was called "Jammin' the Blues" which was made in 1944, but the one I really like is the follow-on in 1950 called "Improvisation."

Improvisation[16] included what I think is the greatest jazz video recording I have ever seen. It starts with a duet with Coleman Hawkins and Charlie Parker. We then meet the rhythm section of Hank Jones, Buddy Rich, and Ray Brown. Bill Phillips then joins the group and finally Lester Young and Harry Edison. Finally, Ella Fitzgerald adds her skat to the music.

This is an amazing 15 minutes of music. I particularly enjoyed watching Charlie Parker, whom I think must have been an incredibly sad man, smiling with pleasure at playing alongside Coleman Hawkins, whom he had never met before. Parker then laughs at the sheer excitement of watching a Buddy Rich solo.

I like to think that only Norman Granz could have brought together such a diverse group of musicians, who clearly enjoyed each other's company. That was the essence of his contribution to Jazz.

This was some of the best-improvised Jazz I have ever heard. A bonus for me was that I had not realized how good a pianist Hank Jones was.

1960s A Time of Change

"Nobody knows where Jazz is going, because nobody has ever known where Jazz was going."[17]

Gary Giddins – Jazz Writer

"Jazz died in 1959. 1959 was the coolest year in Jazz. Jazz has proven itself to be limited, and therefore, not cool. Jazz is dead."

This was written by Nicholas Payton in 2011. Nicholas Payton is an American trumpet player. He is also a prolific and provocative writer who comments on a multitude of subjects, including music, race, politics, and life in America.

Ken Burns in his 2000 Film "Jazz has an interesting perspective. He says there were two major factors which contributed to the decline in Jazz in the early '60s. The first was the "British Invasion," led by the Beatles in 1963 and the second was racial discrimination and race riots.

Oscar Goodstein expressed a more pragmatic view when he closed Birdland in 1965. He said: *"I've had it."*[18] *While the small groups were going too far out, big bands, which usually take a more moderate musical approach, were outpricing themselves."*

It was a time of racial prejudice and political unrest. Among the famous musicians to get actively involved in the politics of the time was **Max Roach** [1924 – 2007] and he was invited to compose a tribute for the centenary of the Emancipation Proclamation, signed by President Abraham Lincoln in 1863. The album was released as We Insist! (subtitled Max Roach's Freedom Now Suite)

Roach said *"I will never again play anything that does not have social significance. We American Jazz musicians of African descent have proved beyond all doubt that we are master musicians of our instruments. What we must do is employ our skill to tell the dramatic story of our people and what we've been through."*[19]

Another quote I really like on this topic is this one by Ornette Coleman: *"You've got to realize. In the western world, regardless of what color you are, what title the music is, it's all played by the same notes."*[20]

17

But some musicians survived, but changed, as they strived to extend the boundaries of Jazz into new areas. In 1961 saxophonist John Coltrane formed a new quartet, utilizing many aspects of Jazz's rhythms and harmonies into his approach, which ensured his position as an important saxophonist and one of the most influential Jazzmen of the decade.

As Jazz struggled to continue through tough times, some jazz musicians looked to the rhythms of rock 'n' roll and strived to add elements of that music to Jazz, creating "fusion Jazz." The culmination of this movement was the landmark recording by trumpeter Miles Davis entitled *Bitches Brew* which became an enormous success and catapulted Davis into almost pop star status.

Jazz in the '60s was taken in another direction by a strong Latin, primarily Brazilian influence. The driving force behind this came from Stan Getz and Joao Gilberto. Gilberto was a Brazilian guitarist and singer, whom Getz invited to New York in 1964 where they recorded "Getz/Gilberto."

The album included "Girl from Ipanema," which later became a worldwide hit when recorded by Astrud Gilberto, Joao's wife. The song was written by Antônio Carlos Jobim, who also composed "Desafinado," which is probably the most recorded Latin Jazz piece of all time.

And yes, there really was a girl from Ipanema. She was Heloísa Eneida Menezes Paes Pinto (now Heloísa Pinheiro) who was just 17 years old at the time. She went on to become a model, a TV presenter and a successful businesswoman. It is hard to believe that it all happened 60 years ago. Nostalgia is to be treasured.

Latin Jazz is still very much alive today, and I will talk more about it in the section on "The Canadian Years."

I recently watched a program on TV and was captivated. It showed highlights of the International Jazz Day[21] 2017[22] in Havana, Cuba. The program included guests: Herbie Hancock, Esperanza Spalding, Cassandra Wilson, Regina Carter, and Kurt Elling, along with some wonderful Cuban Jazz musicians.

One of the highlights for me was to see Chucho Valdes [Born 1941]. A pianist and bandleader, Valdes has led the band *Irakere* for 40 years. It was one of the most exciting jazz events I have seen in recent years.

Tony Carter

1970s A Curious Decade

"One of the things I like about Jazz is I don't know what's going to happen next."

Bix Beiderbecke

Change is always happening. That's one of the wonderful things about Jazz music. That is a phrase used by Morton and Cook[23] in "The Penguin Jazz Guide."

"A vexed and vexing decade" was the view of Eric Porter[24]

Most writers found it a confusing era, but if you look at the key people and the key events, the 1970s made a significant contribution to the future of Jazz. We need to reflect on what was happening at the end of the 1960s to help us understand the 1970s.

Big bands were disappearing because they were too expensive to maintain, there were club closures, declining record sales and ongoing racial tension all led to the need for change. Young Jazz musicians side-stepped into Rock Music, and from there as Morton and Cook put it, *"they moved onto the slippery slope that led to the 'dreaded' fusion"*[25] And perhaps it was a simple as people being bored with bebop.

Maybe the omens were there five years earlier. Let's not forget that Birdland, probably the greatest venue in Jazz history, went bankrupt in 1964, making way for Rock Music.

As Jazz moved away from bebop into the 1970s Latin Jazz already influenced it. That in turn had two streams of music and a Cuban influence joined the Brazilian influence which has started in the mid-1960s.

There was a powerful Afro-Cuban influence. Cuban music had been played in the USA since the 1920's when musicians travelled between Miami and Florida. Later musicians like pianist Chucho Valdes gained popularity. Valdes is still with us, and there are many musicians who were influenced by Chucho Valdes.

So, the influence of Latin Jazz lives on and still has a distinct personality of its own, never having been totally absorbed by American Jazz.

The most dominant influence was Rock Music, creating what came to be called Jazz Fusion. This period offered a wider range of instrumentation with improved technology. In addition to using the electric instruments of rock, such as the electric guitar, electric bass, electric piano, and synthesizer keyboards.

To better understand the power of Rock at that time it is worth remembering that Woodstock took place in 1969. The younger generation, at least, knew where they wanted to go. But Jazz musicians recognized that Rock had a lot to offer them in new instruments. Fusion also used the powerful amplification used by the rock bands.

This led to bass players like **Stanley Clarke** [Born 1951] and **Ron Carter** [Born 1937] competing with guitars in playing solos, not just keeping solid time. Drummers like **Tony Williams** [1995-1997] started to use the big drum kits used by Rock Bands.

The old Fender Rhodes Electric piano made its comeback, often played by **Herbie Hancock** [Born 1940] Chick Corea [1941-2021] and **Joe Zawinul** [1932-2007]

Jazz players were generally better musicians than Rock musicians, and it is so easy to look back now and see what enormous potential Jazz Fusion had. As I look back on that period, I see one event which set the direction for the 1970s. We can thank or blame Miles Davis for that.

Davis was always open to a wide variety of music, and at that time he was influenced by Jimi Hendrix, James Brown, and Sly Stone, and in 1970 released "Bitches Brew", the album which brought legitimacy to Jazz Fusion.

Davis's core working band consisted of Wayne Shorter on saxophone, Dave Holland on bass, Chick Corea on electric piano, and Jack DeJohnette on drums. For Bitches Brew he used a band of twelve, adding Bernie Maupin [Bass Clarinet], Joe Zawinul [Electric Piano] and John McLaughlin [Guitar]

As you will read later, I was never a great fan of Miles Davis and tended to agree with the Jazz purists who protested the blend of Jazz and rock.

Gradually Jazz Fusion matured, became less contentious and gained acceptance. Some of the people behind the new popularity went on to become some of the great names in Jazz. As well as those on the recording we should add **McCoy Tyner** [1938- 2020], **Pat Metheny** [Born 1954], and **Keith Jarrett** [Born 1945]

We also need to look at the influence of Weather Report on Jazz Fusion. The band was founded in 1970 by Joe Zawinul (keyboards) and Wayne Shorter (saxophones) following their experiences in Miles Davis's pioneering electric band of the late 60s,

During the 1970s the band had many highly successful albums and in 1976 were joined by Jaco Pastorius. Heavy Weather (1977) was the album which brought Weather Report to its widest public awareness with the hit single "Birdland".

Pastorius left the band in 1982. Some sources say it was because of clashes with Zawinul over musical direction. Whatever the reason, that probably marked the end of Weather Report as a great band. Shorter seemed to lose interest, and the band broke up in 1986.

But if you look back over the 1970 to 1982 period Weather Report was one of the most successful and most influential bands of any era of Jazz.

Most of my listening was to the Jazz musicians who survived to continue in the style they and we were comfortable with. For those reasons, it was many years later that I first heard Bitches Brew.

Looking back the decade had a confusing start; it produced some amazing musicians to carry Jazz forward[26].

Tony Carter

.

1980's and 1990s Jazz Loses Its Way

"The reward for playing Jazz is playing Jazz." [27]

John Lewis

Jazz, as generally defined, has been with us for about one hundred years. Dividing that period into decades is a little arbitrary, but it doesn't alter the fact that it became increasingly difficult to put a label on the era. The Jazz-rock fusion scene popularized by Miles Davis and his acolytes peaked in the late 1970s, and while it endured subsequent decades, no new dominant scene emerged.

The 1980s were often called the period of Eclecticism. In music theory and music criticism, eclecticism refers to the use of diverse styles, either distinct from the background of an artist using them, or from culturally bygone eras and movements.

In the 1980's the Jazz community shrank dramatically and split. Miles Davis's influence continued, but an older audience retained an interest in traditional and straight-ahead Jazz styles. **Wynton Marsalis** [Born 1961] strove to create music within what he believed was the tradition, creating extensions of small and large forms initially pioneered by such artists as Louis Armstrong and Duke Ellington.

I find Wynton Marsalis something of an enigma. I have read the view of Marsalis's influence as a conservative traditionalist and was a little surprised. Thinking about it, that may be true of much of his work, and he receives a lot of criticism. One example is this quote *'They've done a lot to take the essence of Jazz and distort it; they've put a damper on the main ingredient of Jazz, which is innovation,* 'said George Russell, a much-admired Jazz composer and pianist [28]

It is difficult to separate Marsalis and the Lincoln Centre, so does this refer to the man or the music *"Others say Lincoln Center's institutional heft and commercial muscle has distorted the economics of the Jazz business."* [29]

He has also recorded a lot of music without the Lincoln Centre Orchestra. This ranged from Classical to Ballet. In some of them I see great versatility and innovation.

I still don't understand what drives him, but I tend to feel that he composed and played, more to please himself than his audience.

In the early 1980's, a commercial form of Jazz fusion called pop fusion or "smooth Jazz" became successful and gained significant radio airplay. Smooth Jazz musicians included Grover Washington and David Sanborn. Smooth Jazz also helped to establish or bolster the careers of vocalists including Al Jarreau, Anita Baker, Chaka Khan, and Sade, the last two of whom would not normally be considered Jazz vocalists.

The different worlds met when Chaka Khan's *Echoes of an Era*, which featured Joe Henderson, Freddie Hubbard, Chick Corea, Stanley Clarke, and Lenny White. It also included "And the Melody Still Lingers On (Night in Tunisia)" with Dizzy Gillespie reviving the solo break from "Night in Tunisia".

In 1987, the US House of Representatives and Senate passed a resolution to define Jazz as a unique form of American music stating, among other things, "*...that Jazz is hereby designated as a rare and valuable national American treasure to which we should devote our attention, support and resources to make certain it is preserved, understood and promulgated*":[30]

I see little evidence that anyone took any notice. Government cannot dictate the direction or quality of Jazz Music or any other art form.

Bob Blumenthal makes some interesting points in his article about Jazz in the '80s in Jazz Times[31]. I have sought to paraphrase his ideas.

Teachers at Berklee and Rutgers and the Manhattan School of Music created the era when Jazz education came into its own, even if this meant the systematic standardization of even the most complex techniques[32]. How else can you explain teenagers who could play "Giant Steps" in every key?

What these students lacked was that earlier young musicians had a niche in the music market. Business wasn't paying attention when they graduated, and it took longer for the public to catch up with their work, if ever.

Another idea I liked was put forward Brian Morton in the Penguin Jazz Guide[33]. He talks about the negative impact of the CD on Jazz at that time, and maybe still exists. *The CD gave the industry the opportunity to re-release earlier recordings in a new medium. But because of the extra length they were padded with so-called "bonus" tracks. The bonus consisted of music which otherwise may never have been released.*

The same problem applied to the new, young musicians trying to make a name for themselves. They could not put together an hour's worth of quality music.

Were the 1980's the low point of Jazz? Maybe. My Jazz listening was limited to playing my old favourites: Big Band, MJQ, Dave Brubeck and Wes Montgomery plus the great musicians like Wayne Shorter and Herbie Hancock, who survived, or maybe thrived on Jazz Fusion.

It is noticeable that fewer great musicians were around at this time, and you become very conscious of the people Jazz lost. The 1980's losses included Mary Lou Williams, Thelonious Monk, Earl Hines, Count Basie, Benny Goodman and Chet Baker. There were just not enough up and coming musicians to take their place. If anyone dominated the 1980's, it was the then 19-year-old Wynton Marsalis.

Well, Jazz survived the 1980's, but was still in a very confused state as we moved into the 1990s. Jazz writer, Peter Watrous said of the 1990s[34] *"Jazz burst its seams and fell apart. People said it was a terrible time, and Jazz was in the throes of death. Record companies couldn't sell records, but they kept putting out boring records. Musicians complained about the lack of spaces to perform. It cost too much for young people to come out and hear music, and so on."*

How often over the years did we hear talk like that bemoaning the fact that Jazz was crumbling? Why did no one ask why the younger generation didn't step up to lead the parade? It is not the promoters and producers that create a genre or period of great Jazz. It is the musicians You only must look back at the 1970s to see that.

It was also impossible to follow in the footsteps of the great musicians whom we lost in the 1990s. Here are just some of them: Art Blakey , Sarah Vaughan,, Miles Davis, Dizzy Gillespie, Joe Pass , Ella Fitzgerald, Gerry Mulligan, Milt Jackson, and Harry "Sweets" Edison.

I am going to refer again to Brian Morton again, to try to make sense of the 1990s. *"Nobody quite knew what Jazz was and what it was for[35]"* But this lack of definition did not prevent young musicians from making and recording Jazz. A vast array of recordings flew from the studios, confusing critics, and audiences alike. Morton confesses his confusion by asking *"Was it the best of times? Was it the worst of times? Both perhaps......"*

New names that emerged in the 1990s who went on to achieve success included pianist Brad Mehldau, trumpeters Roy Hargrove and Terence Blanchard, saxophonist Joshua Redman, bassist Christian McBride, and guitarists John Scofield and Pat Metheny. All incredibly talented musicians, with lasting careers ahead of them, but could the phoenix rise again to take Jazz into the 21st Century?

During this period, my interest in Jazz changed. I had moved from England to Canada in 1985 and gradually became increasingly familiar with the Jazz scene here. It was also good to see live music.

There is a section on Jazz in Canada later in the book.

Early Years of the 21st Century

"Jazz is a feeling, more than anything else. It isn't music, it's language"

Eubie Blake

"Reports of the Death of Jazz are Greatly Exaggerated" This is an adaptation of a cable sent by Mark Twain to the press after his obituary had been mistakenly published. It fits well with my views on Jazz in the first two decades of the 21st Century.

This view is echoed by Ken Burns. *"The flame is not out, but it is flickering"*[36]

"The glory days of Jazz are gone, and its remaining heroes are dwindling. The sad truth of my generation is that we must stand by and watch this vital era of music fade into obscurity as its constituents die one by one."[37]

This is a sad commentary but although we did have to watch the greats pass on. But the traditionalists refused to give up their heritage and the music lived on. Among the best-selling albums of 2009 were re-releases of Kind of Blue [Miles Davis], Time Out [Dave Brubeck] and Mingus Ah Um [Charles Mingus]. They were all recorded fifty years ago in 1959.

Jazz in the 21st century is difficult to label. Jazz adapts and reflects the time in which it was created. The countless styles influencing Jazz of this period reveals a rainbow of global cultures, now open to the possibilities of improvisation. There was music for everyone. It was a mix of artists making their way and from *"venerable Jazz greats who refused to go out quietly"* [38]

Here are just a few: Joshua Redman, McCoy Tyner, Stanley Clarke, Chick Corea, Gary Burton, Herbie Hancock, Christian McBride, Hiromi, Brad Mehldau, and some real veterans like: Ron Carter, Ray Brown, and Sonny Rollins.

Genre boundaries will continue to fall apart, and skilled Jazz musicians are perfectly suited to create new music the same way they always have, by standing on the shoulders of their predecessors, while sharing their own modern point of view. And now, a new generation of open-eared audiences is on the same page – categories don't really matter anymore.[39]

Perhaps Duke Ellington's motto is truer now than when he originally said, *"There are only two kinds of music: GOOD music…and the other kind."*[40]

We are now in the early 2020s and still haven't shaken off the impact of the COVID pandemic, and it is still too early to judge its long-term impact on Jazz.

Jazz clubs closed, so live Jazz was missing for two years. In Toronto, several of the clubs that closed have not reopened. Some new ones have appeared but have not yet established a real presence. People go to see live Jazz as much for the atmosphere of their favourite haunt, as well as the musicians.

The Next Generation

"When you begin to see the possibilities of music, you desire to do something really good for people."
John Coltrane –[41]

Sadly, all the musicians I considered for the Greatest ever have one thing in common. None of them are alive today, except Herbie Hancock. Seeing him in Toronto next summer is already in my calendar. Does this mean that you can only get recognition posthumously?

But what will Jazz look and sound like? Thelonius Monk had an interesting view. In an interview when he was asked where he thought Jazz was going, Monk replied "*I don't know where it is going. Maybe it is going to hell. You can't make anything go anywhere. It just happens.*"[42]

Who is going to lead us into the second century of Jazz? Maybe at the top of the list is Saxophonist **Kamasi Washington** [Born 1981] Washington is an awe-inspiring person, as is his music. He came. the fore at the relatively mature age of thirty-seven, but he has made his mark and is here to stay. His expected influence has been compared with that of Wynton Marsalis in the 1980's.

The leading lady is **Esperanza Spalding**, [Born 1984] who is one of today's greatest Jazz talents. The visual impact of her performances is so uplifting. My concern is that she is moving further away from playing the bass towards vocals and dance. " *The Songwrights Apothecary Lab is a gorgeously rendered production that skirts the lines between art rock, free Jazz, and wordless modern creative improvisation.*"[43]

The recording shares its title with a class Spalding teaches at Harvard that is advertised as "half song writing workshop, and half guided research practice" To my mind she is at her best as a Bass player, a view shared by Barack Obama, who invited her to play at the White House on several occasions.

In fact, ladies may dominate the next generation of Jazz Musicians. I predict now that two young lady saxophonists will be amongst them.

Nubya Garcia [Born 1991] was born in London and is the daughter of Caribbean immigrants and as saxophonist, composer, and band leader she is at the heart of London's Jazz renaissance.

Garcia has played around the world, while continually collaborating with new-generation London Jazz leaders like Moses Boyd and Joe-Armon Jones. She has surrounded herself with the Jazz world's top young musician and she has performed and recorded with Makaya McCraven and Shabaka Hutchins She says of herself *"I'm honoured to be called a Jazz musician – I longed for that for so long. But I'm wary of being called a Jazz musician."* [44]

Her influences are far-reaching, playing her sax to rhythms borrowed from reggae and cumbia, a folkloric genre from Columbia. Her debut album *Source* explores her Guyanese and British Trinidadian heritage through compositions that still sound once thoroughly modern.

Camille Thurman [Born 1986] is an American Jazz musician, composer, and member of the Jazz at Lincoln Center Orchestra. She was the first woman to tour and perform full time with Jazz at the Lincoln Centre in the orchestra's 30-year history.

She has released four albums, and more are on the way, including piano-less quintet project with drummer Darrell Green, her husband since January 2021. She is also preparing a set of reimagined Burt Bacharach songs for a major New York show of her own in June at Jazz at Lincoln Center's Appel Room.

She is also a TV performer, and I mentioned earlier that I watched a series of talks about Bessie Smith, which she had written and presented.

Because of her talent and wide-ranging interests, I like to think of her as following in the footsteps of Terri Lyne Carrington.

This is also a great period for vocalists, so let us speculate on who might be this generation's Ella Fitzgerald, Sarah Vaughan, or Abby Lincoln.

Nate Chinen calls vocalist **Cécile McLorin Salvant** [Born 1989] the *"greatest new arrival on the Jazz vocal scene."*[45] Cécile McLorin Salvant earned public acclaim after winning the 2010 Thelonious Monk Jazz Vocal Competition, showcasing classic acoustic Jazz as well as her French heritage[46]

Born in Miami, Florida to a French mother and a Haitian father. She studied classical voice privately before enrolling at the Darius Milhaud Conservatory in Aix-en-Provence, France, where she studied law as well as classical voice.

It will be interesting to see which direction she heads. She further pushed the boundaries of her music with Ghost Song, reinterpreting songs by Kate Bush and Sting alongside her own poetic and original compositions.

Cecile is generally regarded as the top female Jazz vocalist of today. I won't argue too strongly about that, but I would put **Jazzmeia Horn** [Born 1991] ahead of her. I have talked several times about Jazzmeia, and of all the current Jazz vocalists, she has best retained the spirit of Jazz. Bessie Smith, Ella Fitzgerald, and Nina Simone would be truly proud if they could hear her sing.

So exciting about the new musicians we are listening to is the number of successful female musicians, the variety of instruments being played and the number of countries that are contributing to the Jazz scene. Jazz is not dead yet, nor even on its death bed.

Part Two. My Favourite Instruments

"We do not play the piano with our fingers but with our mind."[47]

Glenn Gould[48]

I enjoy Piano and Guitar equally, but for no good reason I am starting with the Piano. It is the variety of styles that the piano offers which makes it such a constant listening pleasure.

The piano was developed in the early 18th century as a successor to the harpsicord. It has been a constant member of Jazz bands from the very beginning. In 1922 King Oliver's pianist was Lil Hardin, who later married Louis Armstrong.

I am going to start with **Ahmad Jamal** [Born 1930-], my favourite pianist, and then talk about others in something of a chronological order.

Ahmad Jamal was born Frederick Russell Jones but converted to the Muslim faith at the age of twenty. He is one of the few musicians who did not start in a band. Most of his career was spend playing in a trio, with the most notable members being drummer, Vernel Fournier and bass player, Israel Crosby. In his book" The History of Jazz"[49], Ted Gioia says this of Jamal *"The charm of Jamal's music came from his ability to maintain the swing, emotional conviction, and mood of his music even when playing the fewest notes?"*

My favourite Jamal recording is "Poinciana." A Poinciana is a beautiful flowering tree, and the song was originally composed in 1936, by Buddy Bernier and Nat Simon

It has been recorded by many notable artists including recorded by Frank Sinatra, George Shearing, Dave Brubeck, Johnny Mathis, Nat King Cole, McCoy Tyner, The Manhattan Transfer, Gerry Mulligan with Chet Baker, and Gary Burton.

But it is the Jamal version which was first recorded on "Ahmad Jamal At the Pershing" in 1958 is probably the most played of the 278 recordings.

35

I don't remember when I first heard the music of **Scott Joplin** [1868-1917]. I can't recall a time when I didn't hear his music. Joplin had died before most of the other musicians in this article were born, but his influence was enormous.

Scott Joplin's legacy reached out to more than just a few artists. Ragtime influenced many styles of Jazz music and Jazz bands. Without Scott Joplin, Louis Armstrong wouldn't have become the musician he became.

Joplin modestly said of himself *"When-I-am-dead in-twenty-five-years-people-are going to begin to recognize me*[50]*"*

Ragtime enjoyed its peak popularity between 1897 and 1918. Ragtime was the first truly American musical genre, predating Jazz. It began as dance music in the red-light districts of American cities such as St. Louis and New Orleans years before being published as popular sheet music for piano. It was a modification of the march made popular by John Philip Sousa, with additional rhythms coming from African music.

The ragtime composer Scott Joplin became famous through the publication in 1899 of the "Maple Leaf Rag" and a string of ragtime hits that followed. His next major success came with "The Entertainer" in 1902. Most people will know this as the theme music from the movie, "The Sting."

After his death in 1917 he was forgotten by all but a small, resolute community of ragtime aficionados until the major ragtime revival in the early 1970s.

I still find it difficult to grasp the magnitude of one person's influence on a musical genre. Everything that is memorable about Ragtime seems to have emanated from Scott Joplin. This is even more remarkable is the fact that there was no recorded music at that time.

Ragtime had several reincarnations, and Joplin's music is still popular. A Canadian pianist called John Arpin [1936 – 2007] was an avid follower of Scott Joplin and I had the pleasure of seeing him on stage for the whole performance of "Ain't Misbehavin" with Jackie Richardson [1947-], one of the great names in Canadian Blues & Gospel music.

All lists of great Jazz pianists include **Art Tatum** [1909 – 1956]. Art Tatum[51] was among the most extraordinary of all Jazz musicians, a pianist with wondrous technique who could not only play ridiculously rapid lines with both hands (his 1933 solo version of "Tiger Rag" sounds as if there were three pianists jamming together) but was harmonically 30 years ahead of his time.

Able to play stride, swing, and boogie-woogie with speed and complexity that could only previously be imagined. Although he was not a composer, Tatum's rearrangements of standards made even the "oldies" sound like new compositions.

My favourite story about Art Tatum is told here, as part of a University of Wisconsin course[52]. *"Tatum was nearly blind and learned to play almost entirely on his own by copying piano roll recordings that his mother played, and he did all of this by ear at the age of three. By the age of six, he was playing music designed as duets, completely unaware that the music was written for two players."*

So many pianists quote Art Tatum as being a major influence on their playing, including Bud Powell, Thelonius Monk, and Oscar Peterson. He was admired by his contemporaries too, hence this quote from Fats Waller *"Folks, I'm only a pianist, but tonight God is in the room…"* His influence extended even further. Charlie Parker was a follower and devotee of Tatum and said, *"I wish I could just play like Art's right hand!"*[53]

I discovered Boogie Woogie very recently, and really find it exciting to listen to. There are three pianists who are always associated with Boogie Woogie in the late 1930s: Meade Lux Lewis, Albert Ammons[54] and my favourite **Pete Johnson** [1904 – 1967]. As a point of interest, Meade Lux Lewis, Albert Ammons were the first musicians to be signed by Alfred Lion, the founder of Bluenote. [1939]. Ammons son Gene was one of Jazz's top saxophone players.

Tony Russell said in his book The Blues – From Robert Johnson to Robert Cray[55] that *"Johnson shared with the other members of the 'Boogie Woogie Trio' the technical virtuosity and melodic fertility that can make this the most exciting of all piano music styles."*

Johnson was more versatile than the other two, being more comfortable in a band setting, and as an accompanist. Part of this may be due that fact that he and his friend Big Joe Turner [56] toured together.

I will talk more about **Oscar Peterson** [1925 - 2007] later in the section called "The Canadian Years", but he deserves a place along with other great Jazz pianists.

After the phenomenal Jazz-piano virtuoso Art Tatum died in 1956, the Canadian pianist Oscar Peterson, who had already been waiting in the wings for a decade, eased his formidable frame on to the throne [57]

There is a story I like which tells how as a 14-year-old he first heard Art Tatum. It is said that he cried and did not play the piano for 2 months," because he did not think he could ever be that good [58]. Oscar Peterson came close to matching Art Tatum and was always strongly influenced by Tatum's music. He later met Art Tatum and they became close friends.

If you like either, or both these great pianists, you will enjoy a discussion [59] about Art Tatum, between Oscar Peterson and Count Basie, recorded in 1980.

Duke Ellington referred to him as "the maharajah of the keyboard[60]." Count Basie said, "Oscar Peterson plays the best ivory box I've ever heard." [61]

However, many critics found Oscar Peterson more derivative than original, especially early in his career. Some suggested that his fantastic technique lacked coherence and was almost too much for some listeners to compute.

Billy Taylor, a fellow pianist, and a Jazz historian, said he thought that while Mr. Peterson was a "remarkable musician," his *"phenomenal facility sometimes gets in the way of people's listening."* I am not sure this is true of great compositions like "Night Train."

He was always in demand with fellow musicians and played alongside giants like Louis Armstrong, Count Basie, Charlie Parker, Nat King Cole, Stan Getz, Dizzy Gillespie, Ella Fitzgerald, and Billy Holiday.

I always enjoyed his playing in a trio to his solo work, and in my opinion his best recordings were made with Ray Brown and Herb Ellis in the 1950s.

A great musician and a great man.

Next on my list of favourite pianists is **George Shearing** [1919-2011]. George Shearing was British and was knighted in 2007 to become Sir George Shearing.

Shearing was born blind, and as a teenager he joined Claude Bampton's[62] band, and he recounts hilarious anecdotes about the trials and tribulations of this all-blind group. By the start of the war years, Shearing was established as one of Britain's most popular and impressive Jazz pianists - broadcasting regularly and playing and recording with **Stephane Grappelli.** [1908-1997]

In 1947 he decided to move to the USA and had his first big hit with "September in the Rain" in 1949. This led to his being invited to play at Birdland, and hence his most famous composition "Lullaby of Birdland," first recorded in 1952. He had been invited by Maurice Levy, the owner of Birdland, to compose an opening piece when Birdland started weekly radio broadcasts.

This concept originated with the Grand Ole Opry which started as a Radio Show in 1925. It wasn't until 1943 that live performances started in the Ryman Auditorium.

Lullaby of Birdland became a standard and lent itself to many interpretations. The many recordings include releases by Quincy Jones, Chaka Khan, Amy Winehouse, Mel Tormé and more. I have not yet brought myself to the point where I want to listen to the Bill Haley and His Comets version ("Lullaby of Birdland Twist)

"Lullaby of Birdland" was also used as the title of his autobiography, published in 2005.

In the 50s he made a name for himself with music derived from swing, bebop and elements drawn from classical music. Shearing's group, which included the distinctive sound of the vibraphone[63], became hugely popular and influential in the 50s.

But like Oscar Peterson, George Shearing was not without his critics. It was said that Shearing seldom played to his full potential. Ted Gioia made a typical comment: "The *"Shearing Sound" was tasteful and inoffensive, but hardly measured the full depth of his talent.*"[64]

I like Jack Kerouac's view of George Shearing. in "On the Road"[65] a scene depicts Shearing on the bandstand. Kerouac notes how *"he began rocking fast, his left foot jumped up with every beat, his neck began to rock crookedly, he brought his face down to the keys, he pushed his hair back, he began to sweat."* The passage continues: *"Shearing began to play his chords; they rolled out of the piano in great rich showers, you'd think the man wouldn't have time to line them up."*

The great versatility of the piano and the pianists can easily be seen by listening to **Ramsey Lewis** [1935 to 2022]. Whenever you listened to a new recording by Lewis, you would discover something different.

We know that he admired Art Tatum and Duke Ellington, but essentially, he developed his own style, incorporating gospel, blues and R&B. Periodically his Jazz music was overtaken by commercial success. *"He thinks beyond category and seems to regard Jazz as part of the continuum of music."*[66]

Ramsey Lewis had been a leader in the contemporary Jazz movement for over 50 years with an unforgettable sound and outgoing personality that allowed him to cross over to the pop and R&B charts.

He released his first recording in 1956, but it was in 1965 that the big breakthrough came with "The In Crowd".

Ramsey Lewis's drummer **Isaac "Redd" Holt** [Born 1932]and bassist **Eldee Young**[67] [1936 – 2007] formed the Ramsey Lewis Trio. They started as primarily a Jazz unit but after their hit, "The In Crowd", in 1965 (the single reached fifth place on the pop charts) Young, and Holt left in 1966 to form the Young-Holt Trio. 'The In Crowd' had moved too far outside their comfort zone.

From 1997 Ramsey Lewis hosted a weekly radio broadcast where he interviewed well- known Jazz musicians. In 2006 Lewis hosted a TV series on PBS[68]. He interviewed a wide range of musicians including Clark Terry, Al Jarreau, Kurt Elling, Pat Metheny, Dave Brubeck, Benny Golson, and Chick Corea. The music is available on You Tube.

Throughout his career, Lewis who is a National Endowment for the Arts Jazz Master, has joined forces with countless other artists to create new and innovative music. You will never fail to enjoy his music.

McCoy Tyner [1938 -2020]. Tyner played professionally in Philadelphia, becoming part of its modern Jazz scene. His neighbours in the city included Bud Powell and John Coltrane.

After high school, Tyner toured with Bennie Golson and Art Farmer and can be heard on their hit record, Killer Joe. In 1960, he became a part of John Coltrane's quartet.

In 1965 Tyner left Coltrane saying *"I didn't see myself making any contribution to that music... All I could hear was a lot of noise. I didn't have any feeling for the music, and when I don't have feelings, I don't play".* [69]

With over eighty albums to his credit and five Grammy Awards, it is difficult to select any one Tyner recording, but I would probably start with "The Real McCoy," from Bluenote

Tyner's energetic style embraces African, Latin, Eastern and bebop rhythms, which have earned him international recognition among the top Jazz pianists of all time. Tyner received the National Endowment of the Arts' Jazz Master Award in 2002 and in 2005, received an honorary doctorate from Berklee College

For me it is the constant variety of styles and influences which make McCoy Tyner such a pleasure to listen to.

Tony Carter

Herbie Hancock. A Special Tribute

I can think of no one who has made such an enormous contribution to Jazz in so many ways.

Herbie Hancock [Born 1940]. Growing up in the '40s and '50s in Chicago, Herbie Hancock was around street vendors, including the "watermelon men," who peddled the fruit. This provided the title and musical inspiration for the song. Hancock wrote: "In reflecting on my childhood, I recalled the watermelon man making his rounds. The wheels of his wagon beat out the rhythm on the cobblestones."[70]

So-called Jazz purists refuse to admit that Watermelon Man is Jazz, but Hancock frequently played it throughout his career to show how important it was, both musically and financially, in his evolution as a musician.

Few artists in the music industry have had more influence on acoustic and electronic Jazz and R&B than Herbie Hancock. As Miles Davis said in his autobiography, [71] *"Herbie was the step after Bud Powell and Thelonious Monk, and I haven't heard anybody yet who has come after him."*

In 1963, Miles Davis invited Herbie to join the Miles Davis Quintet. During his five years with Davis, Hancock and his colleagues Wayne Shorter, Ron Carter, and Tony Williams It's *hard to think of a more significant influence on the small Jazz ensembles of the last four decades than Miles Davis's second quintet* [72]

After leaving Davis, Herbie put together a new band called The Headhunters and, in 1973, recorded 'Headhunters', with its crossover hit single "Chameleon," There are several recordings where Hancock chose to use Chameleon to feature young Jazz musicians.

Herbie also stayed close to his love of acoustic Jazz in the '70s recording and performing with his Miles Davis colleagues, and in duet settings with Chick Corea and Oscar Peterson.

In 1980, Herbie introduced Wynton Marsalis to the world as a solo artist, producing his debut album and touring with him as well.

43

I talked earlier about Herbie Hancock's role in UNESCO. Recognizing Herbie Hancock's "dedication to the promotion of peace through dialogue, culture and the arts," the Director- General has asked the celebrated Jazz musician *"to contribute to UNESCO's efforts to promote mutual understanding among cultures, with a particular emphasis on fostering the emergence of new and creative ideas amongst youth, to find solutions to global problems, as well as ensuring equal access to the diversity of artistic expressions."*[73]

It is impossible to do justice to all the amazing things Herbie Hancock has achieved in his career. Now in the sixth decade of his professional life, Herbie Hancock is still where he has always been: in the forefront of world culture, technology, business, and music. Though one can't track exactly where he will go next, he is sure to leave his imprint wherever he lands.

Much of the information above is taken from the biography on Hancock's own website[74].

Other notable Jazz Pianists

One of the best-known names, not to appear in my choice of Jazz Pianists is **Thelonius Monk** [1917 – 1982]. One of the most influential pianists of the twentieth century, Thelonious Monk had an idiosyncratic improvisational style and made many contributions to the standard Jazz repertoire. He is often regarded as one of the founders of bebop. I know and enjoy "Blue Monk" and "Round Midnight" but have not listened to enough of his music to add him to my list of favourites. The same applies to Horace Silver Errol Garner, Bill Evans, and Hank Jones.

Horace Silver's [1928 – 2014], early influences included the styles of boogie-woogie and the blues, the pianists Nat King Cole, Thelonious Monk, Bud Powell, Art Tatum, and Teddy Wilson, as well as some Jazz horn players. [OBJ]

I have listened to some of Silver's recordings, alongside Art Blakey and the Jazz Messengers, and enjoy his very individualistic style.

Bill Evans [1929 – 1980] has become an entire school unto himself for pianists and a singular mood unto himself for listeners. There is no more influential Jazz-oriented pianist. Only McCoy Tyner exerts nearly as much pull among younger and Evans has left his mark on such noted players as Herbie Hancock, Keith Jarrett, Chick Corea, and Brad Mehldau.

In spring 1958, Evans began an eight-month gig with the Miles Davis Sextet, where he exerted a powerful influence upon the willful yet ever-searching leader. He was deeply involved in the planning and execution of Davis's Kind of Blue album in 1959. Kind of Blue is one of the biggest-selling Jazz albums of all time and has the most moving performances of Evans' life. "Sunday at the Village Vanguard with **Scott LaFaro** [Bass]1936 19613 and **Paul Motian** [Drums] [1931- 2011] Released in 1961, the album is routinely ranked as one of the best live Jazz recordings of all time.

Scott LaFaro [1936 -1961] was sadly killed in a car crash a few days after the Vanguard recording.

The New York Times Essential Library talks about Evan's notion for a new kind of Jazz trio was to have the musicians interact more.

Bespectacled, shy, soft-spoken, and vulnerable, Evans was not a good fit into the rough-and-tumble music business. In part to shield himself from the outside world, he turned to drugs, first heroin, and later, cocaine, which undoubtedly shortened his life.

The oldest of the Jones brothers, **Hank Jones**[75] [1918 to 2010] was a supreme accompanist and underrated soloist. His flexibility and sensitive style kept him extremely busy working in various groups and styles ranging from swing to bebop. He collaborated with vocalists, played in big bands, and played solo, trio, and combo dates.

Jones' earliest influence was pianist **Fats Waller,** [1904-1943] who played in the ragtime stride piano style. As a teenager Jones also idolized **Earl "Fatha" Hines**] and **Teddy Wilson**, [1912-1986] emulating their styles.

Jones' greatest influence was the legendary Art Tatum. Hank was in awe of Tatum's energy, creativity, and flawless technique. Later Jones was able to meet Tatum and watch him through hours of practice sessions.

Throughout his lengthy career, Jones was always in demand. He worked with Jazz at the Philharmonic, then accompanied Ella Fitzgerald from 1948 to 1953. Jones also played many sessions for Norman Granz's labels in the late '40s and early '50s, many with Charlie Parker. He worked and recorded in the '50s with Artie Shaw, Benny Goodman, Lester Young, Milt Jackson, and Cannonball Adderley.

He also played in the **Great Jazz Trio**, originally with Ron Carter and Tony Williams. The trio again backed some great names of Jazz: Art Farmer, Benny Golson, and Nancy Wilson.

Jones was always willing to adopt new styles, and because of that he played with about every major Jazz musician in their time. He had great insights into the players and their music, and I strongly recommend an interview with him conducted by Ben Ratcliff[76] in 2005.

A Note on Duke Ellington

Both Duke Ellington and Count Basie were excellent pianists, but I have excluded them from this section because they a primarily band leaders. Nonetheless, I must talk about an album called "Money Jungle" It was recorded in 1962 by Duke Ellington, Charles Mingus, and Max Roach. Ellington rose to the challenge of the two younger and dynamic musicians. His playing is powerful and exciting, and you can see the influences of Ellington's career, including swing and boogie-woogie emerging. This album should be "a must" on everyone's list.

Ladies of the Keyboard

"If you work on your talent, the plans will fall in automatically."[77]
Mary Lou Williams

Over the one hundred years of Jazz, many talented female Jazz pianists have enjoyed fame. They haven't had the acclaim of their male counterparts, but as you will see their popularity has increased. It can be debated, but the tide began to turn with Mary Lou Williams

They deserve special recognition, so let me pay a short tribute to some of the greatest.

Lil Hardin [1898 to 1971] was perhaps the greatest female Jazz musician of the 1920s and 1930s.

She had a formal musical education, but her love was Jazz, and her first major association was with King Oliver. There she met and married Louis Armstrong. She was a huge influence on Armstrong pushing him to become a solo artist.

During the 1930s, Hardin continued performing as a leader and soloist. It is important to note that during this period, Black women were especially relegated to singing or dancing in a chorus line, but by this point in her life, Hardin successfully established a serious career as a respected Jazz composer and artist. She was a pioneer.

Mary Lou Williams [1910 to 1981] was an American Jazz pianist, arranger, and composer. She wrote hundreds of compositions and arrangements and recorded more than one hundred records. She wrote and arranged for Duke Ellington and Benny Goodman, and she was friend, mentor, and teacher to Thelonious Monk, Charlie Parker, Miles Davis, Bud Powell, and Dizzy Gillespie.

Mary Lou was a brilliant pianist, even being compared with Art Tatum, but it was as an arranger that she made her greatest contribution. An article published by NPR, a broadcasting company, was entitled "How Mary Lou Williams Shaped the Sound of The Big-Band Era"[78]

She was born too early to get the fame she deserved, but today she ranks in the great names of Jazz.

Marion McPartland [1918-2013] was British born, but resident in the US from the end of the Second World War. McPartland arrived as the wife of American GI and trumpeter Jimmy McPartland, whom she had met while playing for the troops in Belgium the previous year.

Soon after her arrival, McPartland befriended the most influential female instrumentalist in Bebop, her fellow pianist Mary Lou Williams. They became lifelong friends. Her first big success came when she led a fine trio including Joe Morello, the percussionist, soon to become famous with Dave Brubeck.

NPR [National Public Radio] began broadcasting Marian McPartland's Piano Jazz, with the host interviewing her guests from the keyboard. Artists and performers as different as Dizzy Gillespie, Steely Dan, and the emerging young star Geri Allen were among the guests.

Most of the notes are taken from her Obituary in the Guardian. [OBJ]She once delivered a solo at London's Pizza on the Park in the 1990s and announced mock-defensively: *"I made that record 40 years ago. "That's when we bought it,"* declared a couple in the front row.[79]

Alice Coltrane's [1937-2007] interest in gospel, classical, and Jazz music led to the creation of her own innovative style. Her talents were expressed more fully when she became a solo recording artist. Her proficiency on keyboard, organ, and harp was remarkable.

Although mainly remembered for her harp playing Alice would collaborate and perform with Kenny Clarke, Kenny Burrell, Ornette Coleman, Pharaoh Sanders, Charlie Haden, and Jack DeJohnette.

She replaced McCoy Tyner as pianist with the John Coltrane quartet and continued to play and record with the band until John died in 1967.[80]

Sadly, she and John had a short marriage [1965 to 1967] Alice and John Coltrane married in 1965. Together they embarked on a deeply spiritual journey of musical exploration. They also brought an exceptionally talented son, Ravi Coltrane, into the world.

Jazz history has many apparently simple anecdotes, but some of them had an enormous impact on what was to come. Alice Coltrane joined her husband's band as a pianist. The New Yorker [81] noted that John had ordered a harp to add to his music, but the instrument didn't arrive until after his premature death.

Despite her grief, Coltrane began to play the harp, resulting in the beginning of an unparalleled Jazz legacy.

Geri Allen [1957 to 2017 first came to prominence in the 1980's, when she moved to New York after receiving a master's degree in ethnomusicology from the University of Pittsburgh.

She also established a long association with the bassist Charlie Haden and the drummer Paul Motian, both veterans of the Jazz avant-garde of the 1960s and 1970s, and played with the drummer Tony Williams and the bassist Ron Carter, former members of Miles Davis's quintet.

Geri Allen was the rare Jazz musician of her generation to have an academic background in musicology as well as in Jazz performance. She went on to spend 10 years as an educator at the University of Michigan, becoming a sought-after mentor to young musicians, and in 2013 she returned to the University of Pittsburgh as the director of its Jazz studies program.

She also used her academic background to research the repertoire of Mary Lou Williams, a pioneering pianist, and in 2006 released the album "Zodiac Suite: Revisited," reinterpreting Williams's famous work. [82]

Allen married trumpeter Wallace Ron**ey** in 1995. Their son Wallace Roney Junior is a brilliant trumpeter, with a growing reputation.

I first heard Geri Allen in the latter part of her career, when she worked with an informal trio called ACS. The other members of the trio were Terri Lyne Carrington and Esperanza Spalding, two of my favourite musicians. What amazing talent.

Renee Rosnes [83] [84] [Born 1962] is a Canadian pianist, although it is hard to claim her for Canada, as she moved to New York City from Vancouver in 1986. It is not difficult to understand why she made that decision. Jazz in Canada was past its 1970s great era, and she was followed over the years by many talented musicians.

Few Canadians have made a mark on the American Jazz scene, but the great ones achieved success. She quickly established a reputation for herself, touring and recording with such masters as Joe Henderson, Wayne Shorter, J.J. Johnson, and bassist Ron Carter.

Over her 30-year career, Rosnes has collaborated with a diverse range of artists, and was instrumental in developing the careers of younger musicians such as Christian McBride, Chris Potter, and Nicholas Payton.

Renee often performs with her husband, acclaimed pianist Bill Charlap.

Renee is also the music director for **Artemis**, an international band featuring the vocalist Cécile McLorin Salvant, clarinetist Anat Cohen, trumpeter Ingrid Jensen, tenor saxophonist Melissa Aldana, bassist Noriko Ueda and drummer Allison Miller.

Renee Rosnes says *"As each year goes by, I see more young female musicians who play all the instruments at an extremely high level. You can see how dedicated they are, and you know they will succeed"* [85]

It is interesting that another Canadian has taken a similar approach in promoting young female musicians. Jane Bunnett has a passion for Latin Jazz. She leads a group of Latin ladies called **Maqueque**.

Eliane Elias [Born 1960] is one of the great international musicians. Elias blends her Brazilian roots and distinctive voice with her virtuosic instrumental Jazz, classical and compositional skills. She herself says that the piano is her first love.

Because it was such an important event in her life and for the world of Jazz, I want to start with something very recent. Elias' 2021 album Mirror Mirror was a lifelong musical dream come true, an extraordinary series of piano duets, partnering of Eliane Elias with the legendary Jazz great Chick Corea, and famed Cuban pianist Chucho Valdés. It is a beautiful album, and this is how Eliane described the experience.

"The album title is about two pianos facing each other like a beautiful mirror image, and how in each duet we reflected each other's thoughts and ideas back and forth. To me, the piano is an extension of my body, heart and soul and is at the center of everything I do. I will always be proud and grateful for the opportunity to have registered these special musical encounters with these two master musicians." [86]

In 1981, she headed for New York. Her first solo album was a collaboration with Randy Brecker in 1984. She and Randy married shortly after that. They were later divorced, but did have a daughter; singer/songwriter Amanda Brecker

The sheer versatility of her work makes it impossible to do justice to her career, so here are some short snippets.

Long known for her native feel of Brazilian music," I Thought About You" truly confirmed Elias' expertise as an interpreter of American standards. It" reached number 1 album in the U.S. and France

She is also considered one of the great interpreters of Antônio Carlos Jobim's music. Elias has recorded two albums solely dedicated to the works of the composer.

The New York Times has described Elias' live concert as "a celebration of the vitality of a culture overflowing with life and natural beauty"[87] and Jazziz magazine proclaimed her, *"a citizen of the world"* and *"an artist beyond category.*[88]

Hiromi Yasuhiro "Hiromi" [Born 1979] is a composer and pianist. She is known for her virtuosic technique, energetic live performances, and blend of musical genres such as stride, post-bop, progressive rock, classical and fusion in her compositions.

She played the piano from the age of six and first great Jazz opportunity came in 1987 when Chick Corea came to Japan and invited her to play a concert performance with him.

It was probably this event that inspired Hiromi to enroll at the Berklee School of Music. During this time, she had the opportunity to meet Ahmad Jamal, and she also had the opportunity to play with Oscar Peterson.

It is impossible to define her style and she herself says you shouldn't try. *"I don't want to put a name on my music. Other people can put a name on what I do. It's just the union of what I have been listening to and what I've been learning. It has elements of classical music, it has some rock, it has some Jazz, but I don't need to give it a name"*[89]

Hiromi gives energetic live performances, and to watch her adds a whole new dimension to her music. It is wonderful to watch the sheer joy she gets from performing. She has a very entertaining blog on her website, and she gives an interesting insight into the difference between studio recording and a live performance.

She is writing about a concert she had just played with Stanley Clark[90] and Lenny White[91]. She says: *'It's vastly different from the concept of CD. Stanley's paintings that he wants to draw are completely different between the studio and the live performance.'*

The recording of "Jazz in the Garden" is one of my favourite albums, being a beautiful blend of the styles of three wonderful musicians.

Guitar

"I never practice my guitar.... from time to time, I just open the case and throw in a piece of raw meat.[92]
Wes Montgomery*"*

The guitar has a far simpler construction than the piano, but talented players over the years have used it to create an enormous variety of very personal styles. Here are some of my favourites.

I had never listened to **Charlie Christian** [1916 – 1942] until recently, although I was aware of the enormous influence he had on future generations of guitarists.

Christian was an important early performer on the electric guitar and a key figure in the development of bebop and cool Jazz. He gained national exposure as a member of the Benny Goodman Sextet and Orchestra from August 1939 to June 1941. I recently discovered a compilation album[93] of various Christian recordings from the Goodman period. It includes his first recording; "Flying Home." It makes wonderful listening, and it is so good to hear Lionel Hampton as part of the Benny Goodman sextet.

He helped bring the guitar out of the rhythm section and into the forefront as a solo instrument. George T. Simon[94] called Christian *"the best improvisational talent of the swing era."*

Christian's influence reached beyond Jazz and swing. In 1990, he was inducted into the Rock and Roll Hall of Fame as an Early Influencer.

Sadly, he died in March 1942, at the age of twenty-five. I find it amazing that one man can have achieved so much in such a brief time.

It is equally impossible to omit **Django Reinhardt** [1910 – 1953]. I don't enjoy his music as much as I did a few years ago. It seems dated, but it is good to listen to him occasionally, just to remember the unique style.

Most Jazz enthusiasts know the story of the gypsy, Django Reinhardt; how he lost two fingers rescuing his wife from a caravan, which he had accidentally set on fire.

As well as remembering "Django" as a soloist, everyone remembers his unique partnership with the French violinist Stéphane Grappelli [1908 – 1997]

What is less well known is the impact of Louis Armstrong on Reinhardt. Guitarist Martin Taylor[95] said, "*Whenever I meet guitarists who tell me that they would love to play like Django, I tell them to listen to Louis Armstrong. That is what Reinhardt did.*"

Another story I like is from when he played with Duke Ellington. Django arrived late for a concert and without his guitar. Ellington found an electric guitar for him. He had never played an electric guitar before but was instantly able to play it. Many of his fans called him "Judas" for deserting the acoustic guitar.

Sadly, Django Reinhardt was another musician dying before his time. He was forty-three.

My favourite Jazz guitar player is **Wes Montgomery** [1923 – 1968]. Montgomery picked up guitar at the relatively late age of nineteen and began teaching himself how to play by imitating recordings of his idol, Charlie Christian. He played locally with his brothers Monk on bass and Buddy on piano[96] before touring the Midwest and South with his own group.

In 1948, he began a two-year stint with Lionel Hampton's big band, a band that included Charles Mingus on bass.

Much has been written about Montgomery's unique way of playing, but what impacts me more is that his approach to music had always been one of feeling rather than one of technique. His inability to read music led to his development of a fine ear; he heard music rather than saw it on a page.

And this was most important in his relationship with his audience. "*Wes believed that the music should be communicated, that the audience was part of the band, and the feeling of the music was more important to him than playing every note correctly.*" Jimmy Stewart wrote in Guitar Player[97].

Regardless of the style of, or the audience for, the music, Montgomery played with feeling and conviction.

The great Jazz guitar player, Joe Pass said *"To me, there have been only three real innovators on the guitar—Wes Montgomery, Charlie Christian, and Django Reinhardt,"* as cited in James Sallis's The Guitar Players.[98]

Montgomery was reputedly a happy smiling man who enjoyed the company of other musicians. He played duos with Milt Jackson and organist Jimmy Smith. Just to look at the album covers will show you how much Wes Montgomery enjoyed his company and the music.

He recorded so many great albums, but one of the best the best is "Smokin' at the Blue Note [1963]. The album combines guitarist Montgomery with the Miles Davis rhythm section from 1959–1963 of Wynton Kelly, Paul Chambers, and Jimmy Cobb.

One of my favourite recordings is "Misty," written by Errol Garner. The YouTube video[99] is a delight to watch.

In December 1961, Milt Jackson collaborated with Wes Montgomery to create the album *Bags Meets Wes*. A Jazzman who was as opinionated as he was gifted, Jackson wouldn't hesitate to share exactly what he thought of a musician, so when he praised Montgomery, one knew his praise was genuine[100].

Sadly, Wes Montgomery died of a heart attack, aged forty-five

Next is **Barney Kessel** [1923 – 2004]. He started as a busy studio musician in Los Angeles but was always in demand for Jazz recordings. He toured with the Oscar Peterson Trio for a year (1952-53) and then, starting in 1953, led an impressive series of records that lasted until 1961 including several with Ray Brown and Shelly Manne.

Kessel recalls the meeting with Charlie Christian which made him determined to become a professional musician. Barney recalls. *"He sat in and played. Later that night he drove me around in his car, took me to a restaurant, talked to me at great length, and was altogether friendly and helpful with advice. That was the only time I met him"*[101]

He was probably at his best during this time and a measure of his success was in 1961 when Gibson manufactured Barney Kessel artist signature guitars.

I have always enjoyed listening to Barney Kessel and it was the influence of his Blues background that made him so easy to listen to. Nesuhi Ertegun better described[102] his style as *"the blues he heard as a boy in Oklahoma, the swing he learned in his first band jobs, and the modern sounds of the West Coast?"*

It is difficult to choose a favourite Barney Kessel recording, so I think I would suggest listening to "To Swing or not to Swing." recorded in 1955 with Harry " Sweets" Edison, Red Mitchell, and Shelly Manne.

I must include **Les Paul** [1915 – 2009]. I first heard Les Paul in the 1950s playing with his wife Mary Ford. One of my favourites was "World is Waiting for the Sunrise" I did not realize at that time just how much Les Paul had contributed to world of music.

Les Paul was determined to be a musician, despite his early musical ability not being superb. *"Your boy, Lester, will never learn music,*[103]*"* one teacher wrote to his mother. But nobody could dissuade him from trying, and as a young boy, he taught himself the harmonica, guitar, and banjo.

Coupled with Paul's interest in playing instruments was a love for modifying them. At the age of nine, he built his first crystal radio. At 10 he built a harmonica holder out of a coat hanger, and then later constructed his own amplified guitar.

Later, with the help of Epiphone, he developed a solid-body electric guitar. It paled in comparison to what Paul would develop with Gibson years later. He always looked for ways to create a fuller, richer sound.

The latter part of Les Paul's career is symbolized by his Monday Night gig at the Iridium Jazz Club in New York. This was a weekly event from 1996 until his death in 2009.

I was determined to see Les Paul, and about two years before he died, I and my family went to the Iridium. He was ninety-two at that time, and was a wonderful host, both to the diners, and a host of young musicians he introduced and encouraged. After the show he would sit and chat with anyone who wanted to talk. That was probably the greatest Jazz experience of my life.

The anecdotes in the notes above are based on an article [104] which was published in Guitar World on the 105th anniversary of Les Paul's birth. The entire article is well worth reading, as it picks out some of the recordings and concerts that gave its audiences such pleasure.

Ed Bickert [1932- 2019] was probably the greatest Canadian Jazz Guitarist ever. He seldom left Canada but gained an international reputation.

Before joining Paul Desmond in 1970, Bickert spent 20 years as perhaps the city's top guitar accompanist. For all his stature as a player, Bickert displayed a modest, soft-spoken, and self-effacing persona, and was a reluctant star. It wasn't until he was in his forties that he first recorded under his own name. *"I've always been a bit — well, more than a bit — apprehensive,"* he told the Toronto Star in 2012. He was also famously quoted as saying, *"I was born to be a sideman."* [105]

He was a member of bands led by clarinetist Phil Nimmons, trombonist Rob McConnell, and flautist Moe Koffman.

Bickert was one of the few Jazz Musicians to retire. He did so in 2000, Nevertheless, his influence was undiminished, especially in his home country.

"Jazz guitarists around the world rightly revere Ed Bickert," Montreal guitarist Mike Rud told The Ottawa Citizen's Peter Hum. *"But for Canadian Jazz guitarists, I think he was the very voice of impeccable musical judgment—when to play, when not to."* Ed Bickert ranks alongside Oscar Peterson as one of Canada's greatest Jazz musicians.

Joe Pass [1929 – 1964].is a new addition to my list of favourite pianists. I often heard him on Jazz FM, Toronto's Jazz Music station as I was driving to and from the college, where I was teaching. But that is not really listening.

I now listen, or more frequently watch videos of Joe Pass. I cannot think of anyone who is a better guitar soloist.

Pass spent much of the 1950s in prison, in hospitals, and half-way houses because of his drug addiction, and it wasn't until the early 1970s that his career took off. Norman Granz, who helped so many musicians in their career, signed Pass to his Pablo recording label.

At that time Granz was managing Ella Fitzgerald. She and Joe Pass made several albums together. They also played concerts as a duo. A video I enjoy very much is "Stormy Weather" performed in Hannover in 1975[106]

New York magazine said of him, *"Joe Pass looks like somebody's uncle and plays guitar like nobody's business. There is a certain purity to his sound that makes him stand out easily from other first-rate Jazz guitarists."*[107]

Vibraphone

"I like the sparkle of the vibraphone."
Evelyn Glennie[108]

I was surprised when I learned that the vibraphone was invented in the 1920s. I first heard vibes in Jazz played by **Lionel Hampton** [1909 to 2002]. He got his start in the 1930s when Benny Goodman introduced the vibraphone into his orchestra.

Hampton started his own band in 1942. During the remainder of the decade, Hampton's extroverted orchestra was a big favorite, leaning toward R&B, sometimes getting exhibitionistic. Among his sidemen, were Dexter Gordon, Charles Mingus, and Wes Montgomery. Hampton's popularity allowed him to continue leading big bands off and on into the mid-'90s, although the 50s were probably the greatest years.

Hampton appeared and recorded with many all-star groups in the 1950s including reunions with Benny Goodman, meetings with the Oscar Peterson Trio, Stan Getz, and as part of a trio[109] with Art Tatum and Buddy Rich.

One of my favourite Hampton recordings is of the Benny Goodman classic "Sing, Sing, Sing," but for Lionel Hampton at his absolute best watch his 1957 recording of "Flying Home"[110]. This was written by Goodman and Hampton in 1942.

Hampton said of himself *"I am motivated. The spirit hits me, and I just keep going and don't stop. The more I play, the more I can invent, the more ideas come to me."*[111]

Much as I enjoy Lionel Hampton, he must remain as my number 2 behind **Milt "Bags" Jackson** [1923 – 1999]

In his biography of Milt Jackson, Scott Yanow[112] said: *"Milt Jackson did for the vibes what Dizzy Gillespie did for the trumpet -- revolutionize its approach."* He slowed the speed on the instrument's oscillator, changed its vibrato and perfected slow, cleverly paced blues solos.

Although best known for his work with MJQ, Jackson started his career with Dizzy Gillespie. He then led his own quintet for a while and it was with that group, he first recorded "Bag's Groove" in 1952. It also became the title of an album Jackson made with Miles Davis.

Jackson loved playing with other musicians. One of my favourites is an album called "Bags meets Wes," which he recorded with Wes Montgomery. He made recordings with John Coltrane, Coleman Hawkins, and Ray Brown.

Milt Jackson is extremely high on my list of "Best Jazz Musician of All Time."

The third and final member of my vibraphone trio is Gary Burton [Born 1943].

He emerged in the 1960s and despite a flourishing solo career, he continued to work as a sideman, touring with George Shearing's quintet in 1963. He also gained fame while with Stan Getz's piano-less quartet from 1964 to 1966 and then put together his own groups. In 1967, with guitarist Larry Coryell, he led one of the early "fusion" bands. Later members of the group included John Scofield and Pat Metheny.

I like his "Departure" album which was recorded in 1997 and covers a variety of Jazz classics. A review of Tribute to Hamp, Red, Bags and Cal" on the Concord website [113] summarizes Burton's place and his awareness of the importance of his predecessors.

He includes Lionel Hampton, and Red Norvo (both pioneers of the instrument in Jazz), Milt "Bags" Jackson (who brought a lyrical approach to the vibes), and Cal Tjader (who made the vibraphone important voice in Cool and Latin Jazz.

How Jazz Musicians Listen to Music

"Anyone who understands Jazz knows that you can't understand it.
It's too complicated. That's what's so simple about it."
–Yogi Berra[114]

As a lecturer, I frequently introduced what I called a "digression." Strictly speaking it was not a digression, but I had reached a point where I needed to stop the flow of teaching to pull together themes or ideas which were related.

I feel the need to do that here and draw some general conclusions that I have reached at this point in my reading and listening.

I am indebted to Ben Ratcliff, Jazz Critic for the New York Times, as many thought-provoking ideas arise from the interviews in his book "The Jazz Ear"[115]

The first thing that struck me was how wide an interest in other aspects of music Jazz musicians have.

Wayne Shorter is a great admirer of the British Composer, Ralph Vaughan Williams, and played his music as student at New York University. In later years he composed music for Renee Fleming, the Opera singer, who has a great love of Jazz music and enjoys singing it.

I was surprised to learn that Pat Metheny was a great admirer of Glenn Gould, the great Canadian pianist, and perhaps just as surprised that it was Gary Burton who first insisted that Metheny listened to Gould.

The next thing I noticed was that all the musicians are admirers of other musicians. The names Miles Davis, Charlie Parker, John Coltrane and above all Art Tatum came up repeatedly.

Hank Jones added greatly to my understanding of Art Tatum. He said that you must not copy the music of someone you admire. Any competent musician can do that, but it lacks inventiveness and creativity. Tatum was inventive and creative at the same time. "*Simultaneous competition you might say*"[116]

The thing that struck me most was the discovery that Jazz musicians tend to listen to Jazz music in a unique way to me. Maybe I shouldn't have been surprised, but they listen to the technique and style and admire it. I listen to the effects and enjoy it.

This leaves me with the question as to whether you must understand Jazz to enjoy it fully, or whether the analytical approach detracts from the pure love of the sound.

Part Three. The Rest of the Band

"I used to look at these pictures of trumpeters pointing their instruments to the ceiling. Stunning pictures, but if you play the trumpet and point it upwards, all the spit comes back into your mouth![117]"

Humphrey Lyttleton

Trumpet

In the early days of recorded Jazz, the 1920s and 1930s, trumpeters led most Jazz bands, often two. In 1923 Joe "King" Oliver invited a young Louis Armstrong to join his band as the number two trumpet.

"The trumpet was probably the dominant solo Jazz instrument until the time when the saxophone, through the influence of Charlie Parker displaced the trumpet as the most glamorous of the horns"[118]

Any discussion of the trumpet must include cornet player, **Buddy Bolden** [1877 – 1931]. Bolden's band was said to be the first to have brass instruments play the blues.

From 1900 to 1906, the Buddy Bolden Band was the top draw in New Orleans. During this time, he ravenously pursued two interests: alcohol and women. But Bolden hit a wall in 1906. Depression, hopelessness, and the allure of alcohol brought on bouts of severe headaches and paranoia (an erratic fear of his cornet probably didn't help his music).

His condition worsened and he was sent to the lunatic asylum which remained his home for more than 25 years, before he died in a state of utter dejection and insanity.

The notes above are based on a biography of Buddy Bolden[119] on the All about Jazz website.

There are no surviving recordings of Buddy Bolden playing, but the memories and stories survived, over the years various tributes have been paid by Sidney Bechet, Jelly Roll Morton, Duke Ellington, Wynton Marsalis and in a song called "Hey Buddy Bolden" by Nina Simone.

In 2019 a Film called "Bolden" [120] was released. Bolden's music was arranged and played by Wynton Marsalis. *"The blowingest man since Gabriel"* *-Jelly Roll Morton* [121]

Louis Armstrong [1901 – 1971] is without doubt the best-known of all Jazz trumpeters. Ross Porter says " *Louis Armstrong has been called the most influential musician of the 20th Century. His magnificent career as a trumpet player, singer and band leader has made him a legend, and his influence on Jazz and popular music cannot be overstated"* [122]

Trumpeter Digby Fairweather said that *"Louis Armstrong was the Shakespeare of Jazz.* [123]

A measure of his talent was that, in 1918, he replaced Oliver in Kid Ory's band, then the most popular band in New Orleans. In 1926, Armstrong finally switched from the cornet to the trumpet.

Louis Armstrong formed his Hot Five, and from 1925 to 1928, Armstrong made more than sixty records with the Hot Five and, later, the Hot Seven. Today, these are generally regarded as the most important and influential recordings in Jazz history; on these records, Armstrong's virtuoso brilliance helped transform Jazz from ensemble music to a soloist's art.

Though his popularity was hitting new highs in the 1950s and being a hero to the African American community for so many years, Armstrong began losing his standing with parts of the Jazz community.

Bebop continued to thrive. Featuring geniuses such as Dizzy Gillespie, Charlie Parker and Miles Davis, the younger generation of musicians saw themselves as artists, not as entertainers.

They saw Armstrong's stage persona and music as old-fashioned and criticized him in the press [124]. Armstrong fought back, but for young Jazz fans, he was regarded as an out-of-date performer with his best days behind him. Armstrong proved them wrong and enjoyed another 20 years of success, perhaps more as an entertainer than a pure Jazz musician.

On 16 August 1956, there began one of the most unlikely partnerships in Jazz. Norman Granz decided to put his star singer, Ella Fitzgerald in the studio with Louis Armstrong to sing duets. It was a bold idea, and one that paid off, as one of Jazz's greatest duets was born.

His success continued with "Hello Dolly," recorded in 1964, replacing the Beatles at Number 1 on the Billboard charts. "What a Wonderful World" was released in 1968, just three years before his death.

I suspect younger people may remember Louis Armstrong for these great hits and are unaware of the amazing contribution he made to the history of Jazz.

You may wonder why **Harry "Sweets" Edison** [1915 -1999] is next on my list of Jazz Trumpeters. The answer is simple. Harry Edison is my favourite Jazz musician of all time. My favourite album "Sweets" was recorded in 1956, and I have probably played it more than any other recording in my collection.

I am not alone in admiring Harry Edison. Here are tributes from two great musicians.

"Nobody else even approaches the trumpet like Sweets. Never too much, but always plenty. He's the greatest trumpet player to play along with singers. He exactly knows how to play with you, how to answer you about what you just sang." [125] Ella Fitzgerald

"Sweets [Edison] can say more with one note than any other Jazz player alive... an approach that stresses simplicity, a glorious tone, natural potency, and an unmatched affinity. He is a unique stylist in our music." [126] Oscar Peterson

Edison had a great start to his career, playing with Count Basie from 1938 to 1950. He later became a member of Jazz at the Philharmonic.

So, what makes Harry Edison so special? His obituary in The UK Independent said, *"The sound of Harry Edison's trumpet was, after that of Louis Armstrong, perhaps the most instantly identifiable signature in Jazz."* [127]

There are several versions of how he got the name "Sweets." I like the one that attributes it to the tone of his music. Another thing I admire about Edison is his ability to be a soloist and a member of the group. He shares rather than dominates.

He also composed many great pieces of music and never lost the "swing" origins of his career. It never ceases to amaze me that so much of the music of the 1950s is so timeless.

Along with saxophonist Charlie Parker and pianist Bud Powell, **Dizzy Gillespie** [1917 – 1993] was one of the founding fathers of the bebop movement as it took root in New York in the 1940s.

Gillespie was rightly proud of his contribution to Jazz. He wrote "*The music of Charlie Parker and me laid a foundation for all the music that is being played now,*" Gillespie said years later. "*Our music is going to be the classical music of the future.*"[128]

Wynton Marsalis is a great admirer of Gillespie, and he wrote: *"His rhythmic sophistication was unequalled. He was a master of harmony—and fascinated with studying it. Gillespie was so quick-minded; he could create an endless flow of ideas at unusually fast tempo"*[129]

Considered one of the most influential musicians of the 20th century, **Miles Davis** [1926 – 1991] was, with his musical groups, at the forefront of many major developments in Jazz music from bebop onwards. Many musicians rose to prominence working with Davis. Gerry Mulligan, John Coltrane, Cannonball Adderley, Wayne Shorter, Branford Marsalis, J.J. Johnson; Horace Silver, Bill Evans, Herbie Hancock, Chick Corea Ron Carter, and Tony Williams all started their career with Davis.

His career started in 1944 when he was just eighteen. The Billy Eckstine band visited St. Louis. Dizzy Gillespie and Charlie Parker were members of the band, and Davis was brought in on third trumpet for a couple of weeks.

A short while after that, Davis joined Charlie Parker, after Dizzy Gillespie had left the band. One of the interesting things I learned from an exceptionally good biography on the last.fm[130] website is that Davis found it difficult to collaborate with musicians who had drug dependencies, including Parker. Davis had his own drug problems and personal relationship problems in the early to mid-1950s but recovered to make one of the most highly rated Jazz recordings: "Kind of Blue" in 1959.

For the next twenty years, Davis was a leader in almost every new wave of Jazz. He kept the respect and admiration of musicians, but his audience was divided between loyal and disenchanted listeners because of his frequent style changes.

One admirer was his long-time colleague Dizzy Gillespie who said:" *Miles got a mystique about him – plus he is at the top of his profession, and he's got way, way, way more money*" [131] He ignored them, writing: "*To be and stay a great musician, you've got to always be open to what's new, what's happening at the moment.*"[132]

Others took a different view. Wynton Marsalis told us "*that Miles sold out, just wanted to make more money, just wanted to sell more records?*" Ken Burns[133]

Miles Davis was a complex man, and often very intolerant, especially of fellow greats like Parker, Coltrane, and Rollins, but he was a highly intelligent and thoughtful man when it came to an understanding of himself. "*Composing will always be a memory of inspiration; improvising is live inspiration, something happening at that very moment.*"[134]

I must confess right from the start that I don't understand Wynton Marsalis.

Wynton Marsalis [Born 1961] is probably the most recognized Jazz Musician of the 21st Century and certainly one of the most influential, and maybe the most enigmatic.

As a technician he is considered one of the finest trumpeters ever to have played the instrument, having made acclaimed classical recordings and becoming the first person to win Grammy Awards in Jazz and classical music in the same year. He has been awarded a total of nine Grammy awards and a Pulitzer prize.

Yet he seems to be almost universally disliked in the Jazz world. Perhaps the cruelest comment comes from the British journalist, Richard Williams:" *If Wynton Marsalis is its creative figure head, then Jazz is probably really dead this time.* [135] "[136]

Almost as damning is a quote from Jazz Trumpeter, Randy Sandke, "Marsalis does not aspire to be an innovator, and no one else is allowed to have ideas either."

Miles Davis was a little less abrasive, *"I really liked Wynton when I first met him. He is still a nice young man, only confused"*[137].

Chet Baker can be relied on to make a telling comment on almost any topic, *"Well if I could play like Wynton; I wouldn't play like Wynton."*[138]

Is the Jazz world too harsh on Wynton Marsalis? I don't know. But you cannot dispute his talent as a musician, nor the success of the Lincoln Centre Jazz Orchestra

Let us just look briefly at his career. Marsalis decided to leave Julliard to play with Art Blakey and subsequently toured with Herbie Hancock, whose group included Tony Williams and Ron Carter. Marsalis was only nineteen at the time.[139]

Wynton Marsalis is usually painted as a conservative and was extremely critical of the contemporary music people like Miles Davis were introducing. Despite this perception, over his lengthy career he has recorded music in many styles, Latin, religious, and blues, and others obviously for fun, like his recording with Country Music star, Willie Nelson, and appearances on Sesame Street.

Marsalis has been Musical Director of Jazz at the Lincoln Centre for nearly 30 years, and as such it has given him enormous influence over Jazz education and performances. The 15-piece Big Band is certainly the best big band of the last generation.

I discussed Marsalis a little in my section in the 1980's. I enjoy some of his music, but parts of it lose me, and the thought that still goes through my mind as to whether his prime audience is the Jazz Community, or himself.

Hugh Masekela [1939 – 2018) was a South African trumpeter, flugelhornist, cornetist, singer and composer who has been described as "the father of South African Jazz". He deserves a special mention, because of his social conscience as well as his music. He may not be in the Top Ten Jazz trumpeters, but I enjoy his playing and admire the man.

In 1960, at the age of 21, he left South Africa to begin what would be 30 years in exile from the land of his birth. This followed the Sharpeville Massacre.

This coincided with a golden era of Jazz music and the young Masekela immersed himself in the New York Jazz scene. Under the tutelage of Dizzy Gillespie and Louis Armstrong, Hugh was encouraged to develop his own unique style, feeding off African rather than American influences.

"Bra Hugh" met and married **Miriam Makeba**, [1932- 2008] who had been helped in her move to the USA by Harry Belafonte. Miriam, "Mama Afrika," was a singer and was even more politically active than Masekela.

It is difficult to separate their musical and political careers. "Soweto Blues" is pained and melancholic. Hugh Masekela composed the song and lyrics as a tribute to the martyrs of the Soweto Uprising. Miriam Makeba sang the song in 1977. The central question that runs through its chorus: *"Where were the men when the children were throwing stones? Where were the men when the children were being shot?"*[140]

In 1990 Hugh returned home, following the unbanning of the ANC and the release of Nelson Mandela – an event anticipated in Hugh's anti-apartheid anthem 'Bring Home Nelson Mandela' (1986) which had been a rallying cry around the world.

I have not done justice to Masekela's and Makeba's involvement in South African politics during the period of Apartheid. If you are interested, I recommend an article entitled "Hugh Masekela and Miriam Makeba"[141] poet and cultural critic Hanif Abdurraqib for the KCRW music documentary podcast wrote this piece[142] Lost Notes.

Trombone

The first time I heard Jack Teagarden on the trombone, I had goose pimples all over.[143]
Louis Armstrong

The trombone's ancestor was a medieval instrument called the "sackbut." Developed in the 15th century, the sackbut looked quite like the trombone, and became known by a new name: *trombone*, derived from Italian, 'trombone' meaning 'big trumpet'[144]

The trombone was an essential component of the brass parade bands that were a staple of Black social and cultural life in southern cities around the turn of the twentieth century. As these bands evolved into Jazz ensembles, the trombone became an equal partner of the clarinet and cornet. The first Jazz band to record was led by the renowned Creole trombonist, Kid Ory (1922).

The rise of big bands led to trombone sections of four (even five) players and coincided with the emergence of the first major Jazz trombone soloists. Jack Teagarden arrived in New York and raised the trombone playing to new heights of technical virtuosity and soulful expression. He later came to lead his own band.

The demise of the big bands proved to be a setback for the instrument. Over the past fifty years, as smaller ensembles have come to dominate Jazz, the trombone, all too often, has been looked upon as an afterthought[145].

Kid Ory[146] [1886 – 1973] was one of the last survivors of the generation of New Orleans Jazzmen who laid down the foundations of Jazz in the first two decades of the 20th century. He was a self-taught musician who started on homemade banjos and guitar until he had saved $4 to buy a used valve trombone.

At the age of twenty-one moved to New Orleans, the big city. After leading his own band for several years, he moved to Chicago and played with King Oliver, Louis Armstrong's Hot Five and with Jelly Roll Morton's Red-Hot Peppers. In 1926, the Hot Five recorded "Muskrat Ramble," Kid Ory's best-known composition.

A little piece of trivia. The style that Ory and others developed is often called "tailgate trombone." In the early days of Jazz, bandleaders would commandeer horse-drawn furniture wagons, playing to promote that night's gig. Because trombone players had to deal with the action of the long slides of their horns, they'd sit at the tailgate, to give them more room.[147]

Ory found little work in the 1930s but in 1944, an unexpected New Orleans Jazz fan, Orson Welles, who had a weekly radio program on CBS put together a group to on his show[148]. Kid Ory was included in the group and the response of both Welles, and the listeners were so enthusiastic that it became a regular feature. Kid Ory emerged as the band's leader.

. For the next 20 years, Ory and his Creole Jazz Band worked steadily. His final move was to Honolulu where he died at the age of eighty-six.

When I first discovered that Kid Ory recording in about 1956, I had no idea what an important figure in Jazz history I had stumbled on.

Considered by many to be the finest Jazz trombonist of all time, **J.J. Johnson** [1924 to 2001] somehow transferred the innovations of Charlie Parker and Dizzy Gillespie to his more awkward instrument, playing with such speed and deceptive ease that at one time some listeners assumed he was playing valve (rather than slide) trombone. He was the first trombonist in the Bebop era.

He made his recording debut with Benny Carter on "Love for Sale" in 1943, and played at the first Jazz at the Philharmonic concert in 1944. Johnson also had plenty of solo opportunities during his stay with Count Basie's Orchestra (1945-1946). Over the next few years, he played with all of the top bebop musicians, including Charlie Parker, the Dizzy Gillespie big band, and the Miles Davis Birth of the Cool Nonet.

Times were hard for Johnson for a while, but his fortunes changed when, in August 1954, he formed a two-trombone quintet with Kai Winding that became known as Jay and Kai and was very popular during its two years. Johnson played for many years after that, but his innovative playing in the Bebop that was the highlight of his career.[149]

Another fine trombonist to emerge from the bebop era was **Kai Winding** [1922 - 1983] Born in Denmark, Winding moved to the US with his family when he was twelve.

During his career he was always to an extent overshadowed by J.J. Johnson, although they co-led one of the most popular Jazz groups of the mid-'50s.

Winding's first burst of fame occurred during his year with Stan Kenton's Orchestra (1946-47) during which his phrasing influenced and was adopted by the other trombonists, leading to a permanent change in the Kenton sound.

Winding and Johnson were both big band successes and sounded similar at the time. Jay and Kai had an extraordinarily successful 2 years together. But Winding wanted to experiment and led a four-trombone septet through the latter half of the 1950s and into the '60s. The multi-trombone group created a rich sound but had limited commercial success. I cannot think of any trombone player since who could match either Johnson or Winding.

Saxophone

"I would like to thank my father who discouraged me from playing the violin at an early age.
Paul Desmond -.[150]

The Saxophone was invented in 1846 by Adolphe Sax, but it was not until the 1920's that Jazz music began to feature the saxophone. Following it, the saxophone became featured in music as diverse as the "sweet" music of Paul Whiteman and Guy Lombardo, Jazz, swing, and large stage show bands][151]

I should probably say that the Saxophone is my least favourite instrument, and there are some widely acclaimed musicians that I just don't enjoy listening to. Among them are Charlie Parker and John Coltrane.

I do, however, recognize the importance of Charlie Parker and John Coltrane but because of my lack of knowledge of them, I have primarily used the views of other people, who knew them and their music better than me.

Charlie Parker (1920-1955) tops most lists of the best Jazz saxophonists ever is the man fans referred to simply as "Bird". If he had lived beyond 34 years of age, who knows what he could have accomplished. The quote[152] below is typical of biographies of Charlie Parker. Like many people, I probably knew more about Parker and his addictions than I did about his music.

"Charlie Parker was one of the most influential figures in the development of Jazz. He was a troubled man, with drugs and drink at the heart of his problems. He was also a genius, a man of which it can be said, that changed the course of Jazz history"[153]

Because of the importance of Charlie Parker, I decided to try to find out more about the man and his music. One of the first things I found was this delightful quote from Charles Mingus in 1955:

"Life has many changes. *Tomorrow it may rain, and it's supposed to be sunshine 'cause its summertime. But God's got a funny soul, he plays like Charlie Parker.*[154]

In 1942, Charlie began to get serious recognition, but not that everyone "got" what Parker was up to. Some, like Louis Armstrong, didn't get it at all. *"There was none of the smoothness of regular swing bands in what Charlie played; many just heard it as notes in some random order."*[155]

In 1943, Parker played in Earl Hines's band along with Dizzy Gillespie. Gillespie was one of the few stabilizing influences in Parker's life. Hines recalls how conscientious they were. *"They would carry exercise books with them and would go through the books in the dressing rooms when we played theatres."*[156]

It was around this time that Parker first met Miles Davis. It was an uneasy, though very fruitful, relationship. Along with Dizzy, these men created what's come to be called Be-Bop, and in 1949 a new club opened in New York; it was named Birdland in the saxophonist's honor.

The early 1950s was perhaps his best period. He recorded with Dizzy Gillespie, Thelonious Monk, and Buddy Rich. At last, he seemed to be getting his life under control, even if the drugs and booze were never entirely absent. Parker's band was great around this time, featuring a young John Coltrane.

But the good period did not last. Things got so bad that he was even banned from Birdland. By September 1954 Bird had a breakdown; he even attempted suicide. He did get back on his feet and was booked to appear at Birdland in March 1955. Before he could fulfil his engagement, however, he died. Bird was 34 years old. Despite his remarkable success, he died penniless, and in 2005 a saxophone which he had pawned many times was sold for $250,000[157]

I have not heard enough of Charlie Parker to make my own call on how great he was, but I had to listen to more. My starting point was "Yardbird Suite:" recorded between 1946 and 1949.

John Coltrane [1926- 1967] is another saxophonist whose music I don't know very well, so let me try to discover more about John Coltrane the person.

An interesting insight into John Coltrane is provided by Wynton Marsalis on the Ken Burns film "Jazz.' Marsalis describes him as the "*most earnest person you would ever meet.*" He goes on to describe his music as "*warm and spiritual.*"[158]

Marsalis's view was correct. Coltrane grew up in a deeply religious family and in his own later years became deeply religious and spiritual.

His musical career started when he volunteered for the Navy and was assigned to the USA Navy band Melody Masters, but when he was discharged, he never really settled, and sadly became addicted to heroin.

It was Miles Davis who, in 1955, rescued Coltrane, and until 1959 he played alongside Davis, before forming his own band. By the 1960s he was in great demand and probably the highest-paid musician of the day.

Coltrane's 1964 album "A Love Supreme" is regarded as "one of the most important records ever made, A Love Supreme was his greatest studio outing, which at once compiled all of the innovations from his past, spoke to the current of deep spirituality that liberated him from addictions to drugs and alcohol, and glimpsed at the future innovations of his final two and a half years".[159]

One of the good things times of his life was the time Alice was his wife. Although better known later as a harp player, she was a pianist and replaced Tyner McCoy in Coltrane's band.

Stan Getz [1927-1991] was apparently also bipolar which led to great mood swings and his friend Zoot Sims is reputed to have said: "*Yes.*[160] *Stan's a nice bunch of guys.*"

But Getz survived this to create great music. In the early part of his career, he played regularly with Woody Herman, Stan Kenton, and Benny Goodman. I have heard little of his music during this period.

The Stan Getz I know is the period with Joao Gilberto and Antonio Carlos Jobim. The Bossa Nova became popular in Brazil in the late 1950s and Stan Getz was introduced to the music, by bassist Don Payne, who had visited Brazil with Tony Bennett. Getz was captivated by bossa nova and released two albums in 1962.

It was in that same year that Gilberto, Jobim and Sergio Mendes played at Carnegie Hall. Getz was introduced to them, and the rest of the story we know. The Getz/Gilberto album was released in 1964 and is regarded as one of the best ever Jazz recordings.

The '70s and '80s were not his best, but Stan Getz retained a strong following, particularly in Europe. *"No matter what demons might beset him, however, Getz was recognized over his entire career for delivering performances of consistently high quality."*[161] His career ended shortly before his death in 1991 with one of the most beautiful vocal collaborations[162] of his entire career; *You Gotta Pay the Band,* recorded with singer Abbey Lincoln.

Gerry Mulligan [1927 – 1996] was born in the same year as Stan Getz but had quite a different career. His first instrument was the piano, and he was better known as a composer and arranger than as a musician.

On his occasional solos for Gene Krupa, he played the Alto sax, but with Birth of the Cool with Miles Davis he first played Baritone sax.

It was the intriguing sound of the baritone sax that attracted me to Mulligan's playing. It will not surprise you to learn that my favourite pieces were Mulligan compositions like "Walkin' Shoes," "Line for Lyons," and "Bernie's Tune."

Jazz has so many anecdotes associated with it, that it adds to the fun. In the early 1950s Mulligan and **Chet Baker** [1929-1988] enjoyed remarkable success with the "Pianoless" group. There is one version of the origin of this format was that they had a concert the day after Vibraphonist Red Norvo, and that the piano had been removed[163]. Mulligan's version that there was piano, but they didn't want to use it.

Paul Desmond [1924 – 1977] was a key member of the Dave Brubeck Quartet between 1951 and 1967 He wrote the group's most famous tune 'Take Five.'

Paul Desmond is widely recognized as a melodic improviser and as the benchmark of cool Jazz sax players. His warm, elegant tone was one that he admittedly tried to make sound like a dry martini.[164] He and Art Pepper were virtually the only alto players of their generation not directly influenced by Charlie Parker.

Desmond made several recordings after leaving Brubeck. An interesting one is "Bridge over Troubled Water" 1967. With the backing of Herbie Hancock, he interpreted Simon & Garfunkel tunes.

Desmond died on May 30, 1977, not of his heavy alcohol habit but of lung cancer, the result of his long-time heavy smoking. Never without his humour, after he was diagnosed with cancer, he expressed pleasure at the health of his liver. His fans were unaware of his rapidly declining health.

He also recorded with MJQ, but in my opinion Desmond was at his best when playing with Brubeck. The synergy brought out the best of both.

Drums

*Thelonius Monk encouraged me to emancipate the drums from their
subservient role as timekeepers"* [165]
Max Roach

Drums are almost certainly the oldest of all musical instruments.
Drums have been found in China dating back to 5500 BC. The drums
were often used in religious rituals or ceremonies. They have been used
in Jazz since Dixieland in the 1910s, but they underwent a major change
in the 1950s and 1960s.

Influenced by people like Max Roach the role of drums in Jazz took
on a more dominant role. The modern drum set emerged.

Most people regard **Art Blakey** [1919 – 1990] as the greatest of all
Jazz drummers. Blakey started his musical life as a pianist, but a club
owner forced him to hand over the piano and play the drums. The pianist
was a young Errol Garner. A good career moves for both[166].

His early career was phenomenally successful, and he played with
many leading musicians, but the defining moment was probably in 1956
when he and Horace Silver formed the Jazz Messengers.

Blakey played very loud and extremely hard. No drummer ever drove
a band harder, and none could generate more sheer momentum during
a tune. *"He started every performance full-bore and went from there. His style was
relentless, and woe to the young saxophonist who couldn't keep up, for Blakey would
run him over like a fullback."* [167]

. This is a good place to talk about the **Jazz Messengers**. They were
a dominant force over four decades and did not fit into a decade-by-
decade chronology.

The Jazz Messengers existed for over thirty-five years beginning in
the early 1950s and ending when drummer Art Blakey died in 1990

The group evolved into a proving ground for young Jazz talent. Each
iteration of the Messengers included a lineup of new young players.
Having the Messengers on one's resume was a rite of passage in the Jazz
world.

"*Yes sir, I'm gonna stay with the youngsters. When these get too old, I'm gonna get some younger ones. Keeps the mind active.*" [168]Art Blakey, A Night at Birdland,

Many former members of the Jazz Messengers established careers as solo musicians, such as Lee Morgan, Benny Golson, Wayne Shorter, Freddie Hubbard, Hank Mobley Curtis Fuller, Cedar Walton, Keith Jarrett, Chuck Mangione, Chick Corea, Wynton Marsalis, Branford Marsalis, Terence Blanchard and Clifford Brown, Randy Brecker, Slide Hampton, and Tyner McCoy

. A wonderful place to learn.

There were three reasons for the longevity of the Jazz Messengers. Bebop was complex and un-danceable. So, Hard Bop moved back in the other direction. It used simpler melodies that were easier to sing, a slower tempo, a strong backbeat, and a solid bluesy groove, all of which made it very danceable.[169]

The second reason must be the quality of the musicians, with the sound changing a little as new people joined the band. But they stayed true to Hard Bop for the whole time.

The third reason is that the Jazz Messengers toured the world, gaining worldwide popularity and an everlasting presence on the Jazz scene.

At the time of Art Blakey's death in 1990, the Messenger aesthetic dominated Jazz, and Blakey himself had arguably become one of the most influential Jazz musicians of the past 30 years.

It is utterly amazing that one era produced what are probably the greatest Jazz drummers of all time. I am not going to try to compare **Gene Krupa** [1909 – 1973], **Buddy Rich** [1917 – 1987], and 3 **Max Roach** [1927 – 2007]. They were all great drummers and all entertaining to watch. One of the best things about watching drummers is their enthusiasm and the excitement they generate.

I have never seen an introverted drummer.

Gene Krupa is synonymous with a driving drum style and a dynamic sense of showmanship qualities that made the Chicago-born drummer one of the musical giants of the Swing Era. [170]Behind his public image, Krupa was a devoutly serious and self-disciplined musician. As Benny Goodman would recall in his autobiography" Kingdom of Swing," *"No matter how much playing [Krupa] did, he was always working, developing his hands, and getting new ideas."*[171]

Krupa felt it was a disadvantage to be a white Jazz musician, and he met the great New Orleans drummer Warren "Baby" Dodds (1898 – 1959). *"Baby was the band's central strength,"* reminisced Krupa in Drumming Men, *"the way he used the drums, the rims, the cymbals were just marvelous." He was one of my main inspirations."*[172]

By the late 1930s Krupa emerged as a national phenomenon. His work on Benny Goodman's 1936 hit *"Sing, Sing, Sing"* produced the classic drum anthem of the Swing Era, and his appearance on stage and film catapulted him to superstar status.[173]

But the association with Goodman ended shortly after that. *"They had different ideas about how to play music,"* explained band member Lionel Hampton *"Benny didn't like all the crazy antics and sensationalism that he felt were overshadowing the real music. Gene thought the craziness was simply basic showmanship. Although I tended to agree with Gene, I stayed out of it."*[174]

With the demise of big bands during the 1950s, Krupa began performing in small combos and toured internationally with Norman Granz's Jazz at the Philharmonic.

It was during that time he met Buddy Rich, and they made several recordings together. The best known one is "The Drum Battle." It is a highly entertaining piece of friendly rivalry.

Buddy Rich was "arguably the greatest Jazz drummer of all time", according to Drummerworld[175] "The legendary Buddy Rich exhibited his love for music through the dedication of his life to the art. Rich could play with remarkable speed and dexterity despite the fact that he never received a formal lesson and refused to practice outside of his performances."[176]

Rich's Jazz career began in 1937 and by 1939, he had joined Tommy Dorsey's band, and he later went on to play with such Jazz greats as Dizzy Gillespie, Louis Armstrong, and Gene Krupa. Along with Gene Krupa, Rich was regularly featured in Jazz at the Philharmonic.

A long-time friend, Frank Sinatra, presented the eulogy at Rich's funeral. Today, Buddy Rich is remembered as one of history's greatest musicians. According to Jazz legend Gene Krupa, Rich was *"The greatest drummer ever to have drawn breath."*[177]

For fun you may want to watch "The Drum Battle" between Buddy Rich and Sesame Street's Animal.[178]

I talked about **Max Roach** [1927 to 2007] and his then wife Abby Lincoln and their powerful struggle against racial prejudice.

As a young man, Max Roach, a percussion virtuoso capable of playing at the most brutal tempos with subtlety as well as power, was among a small circle of adventurous musicians who brought about wholesale changes in Jazz. He should be considered one of the founders of bebop. He remained adventurous to the end.[179]

He explained his philosophy to The New York Times in 1990: *"You can't write the same book twice. And though I run into artistic crises, they keep my life interesting."*[180]

In Roach's hands, the drum kit became much more than a means of keeping time. He saw himself as a full-fledged member of the front line, not simply as a supporting player, and was accepted as such by his peers and audiences.

As early as the 1940s, he had become a regular presence on the New York Jazz scene, working with Charlie Parker, and Dizzy Gillespie. Within a few years he had become equally successful on record, participating in recordings such as Miles Davis's "Birth of the Cool" sessions in 1949 and 1950.

Roach made the transition from sideman to leader in 1954, when he and the young trumpet virtuoso **Clifford Brown** [1930-1956 formed a quintet. That group, which specialized in a version of bebop that came to be called hard bop, took the Jazz world by storm. But it was short-lived. In June 1956, at the height of the Brown-Roach quintet's success, Brown was killed in an automobile accident. He was twenty-four. The sudden loss of his friend and co-leader, Roach later recalled, plunged him into depression and heavy drinking from which it took him years to emerge.

In 1960, Roach collaborated with the lyricist Oscar Brown Jr. on "We Insist! Freedom Now Suite," which played variations on the theme of Black people's struggle for equality in the United States and Africa. The album, which featured vocals by Abbey Lincoln received mixed reviews. Critics praised its ambition, but some attacked it as overly controversial. Roach was undeterred. Let me repeat an earlier quote from Roach *"I will never again play anything that does not have social significance,"*[81]

Roach continued to play and record, but it is generally thought that by the time he joined the faculty of the University of Massachusetts in 1972, teaching had come to seem an increasingly attractive alternative to the demands of the musician's life. He continued to play, record, compose and teach until 2000.

Tony Carter

A Tribute to Terri Lyne Carrington

"Women have not been socialized to play drums. It's not natural for us to hit things"[182]
Terri Lyne Carrington

Terri Lyne Carrington (Born 1965) is an American Jazz drummer, composer, producer, and educator. She is a musician I greatly enjoy listening to, and a person whom I greatly admire. I think she will have a place in Jazz history, not just because she is one of the greatest female Jazz musicians ever but for her contribution to the Jazz scene and to society.

She has played with Dizzy Gillespie, Stan Getz, Clark Terry, Herbie Hancock, Wayne Shorter, and many others. She has won three Grammy Awards, including a 2013 award for Best Jazz Instrumental Album, which established her as the first female musician to win a Grammy in this category.

Carrington serves as Founder and Artistic Director of the Berklee Institute of Jazz and Gender Justice, and it is important to understand her lifelong commitment to the encouragement of diversity[183]. She expressed her commitment like this. *"I'm fascinated by how we all talk about the things that affect us, and how we, as people and as privileged artists, voice concerns and make change happen." "Dealing with racism has been part of my whole life","*

[184]Carrington has earned a reputation for harnessing music to political and moral themes. The 2013 Money Jungle album dealt with social-justice topics by adding vocals and funk flavors to eight Duke Ellington compositions and two by Carrington herself. Her Money Jungle album came 50 years after the original recording by Duke Ellington, Charles Mingus, and Max Roach.

How does she see herself as a musician? *"I just love playing creatively. I like playing in a small group setting, where I get to kind of play shapes and colours and groove, so I like to try to paint as I play."*[185] In another part of this book, you will see similar comments from Hiromi.

I greatly admire her attitude as an educator. As a lecturer in Leadership, I shared Carrington's philosophy. *"It's important for me to teach because it keeps me current and in touch with what's happening now. I give them advice really to do the same thing, to reach back to the past and understand the history, so that it can really inform what's happening now. I try to make them as prepared as possible."*[186]

Bass

The bass player is the key. He needs to keep a steady pulse, to provide the bottom and to hold the music together[187]
Wynton Marsalis

The Bass is a relative newcomer to the Jazz scene. Bass notes in Dixieland Jazz tended to be provided by wind instruments like the tuba, or even sousaphone. The upright bass became popular in the 1950s through musicians like Ray Brown, Charles Mingus, Paul Chambers and Scott LaFaro.

The electric bass has played a bigger role in blues music, and one of the few great Jazz musicians to play electric and upright bass was Jaco Pastorius]

Double-bassist **Ray Brown** [1926-2002] was a leader in defining the modern Jazz rhythm section. I find reading about Ray Brown is almost like reading fiction. He always seemed to be in the right place at the right time.

His musical education began with the piano but when he discovered how many pianists there were in his school, Brown thought of switching to the trombone, but could not afford a horn. The school orchestra needed a bass player and had an extra bass.

While still in high school, he began playing his newfound trade in Jazz clubs in Pittsburgh. Then *Downbeat* magazine urged him to go to New York. On his first night in the city, he bumped into a friend from the road, pianist Hank Jones, who introduced him to trumpeter Dizzy Gillespie. Dizzy was looking for a bass player and hired Brown on the spot

Joining Brown in the band's rhythm section were Milt Jackson on vibes, drummer Kenny Clarke and John Lewis on piano. The four musicians discovered a cool, comfortable chemistry, and went on to become the Modern Jazz Quartet in 1952. Brown left MJQ to work with Ella Fitzgerald.

He became her accompanist, musical director and in 1948, her husband. The union was short-lived, and the couple divorced four years later, but their personal relationship continued for many years.

In 1949, Ray began an 18-year relationship with Norman Granz' Jazz at the Philharmonic. One of the musicians was pianist Oscar Peterson. It was to be a fateful night at Carnegie Hall. When drummer Buddy Rich bowed out at the last minute, Brown and Peterson were suddenly a duo and their connection made the music ring. Ray went on to play with the Oscar Peterson Trio for 15 years.

The period with Oscar Peterson is what I enjoy most.[188] Along with Ed Thigpen [Drums] they produced wonderful recordings, many of which were standards. For me that combination of music and musicians was irresistible,

Even Brown's passing seemed to fit in with his life. On July 2, 2002, Brown was in Indianapolis, Indiana for a gig. That afternoon, Ray indulged in his favourite activity outside of Jazz: golf. After his round, Ray returned to his hotel to catch a brief nap before preparing to play that night. Ray Brown died in his sleep.

Most of the material above is taken from NPR's excellent profile of Ray Brown[189]

I find **Charles Mingus** [1922 – 1979] to be an enigma. He was born in Nogales, Arizona. He is of Chinese English American descent. He felt that he was victim of racism, and this is reflected in his compositions. He was a giant of a man with an aggressive attitude to match. He was known for his intense on-stage rage and violent personality.

As I read about Charles Mingus my view is that he was a "lost soul." His personal life was a disaster. As a musician his immense talent led him to play with bands without becoming part of the team. A period of stability came when he had his own band. It was with that group of players he recorded " Mingus Ah Um," arguably the best Jazz recording by a bass player.

Part of his enigmatic character was that Mingus was not always heard. He preferred to compose and to be the leader of the band over playing solo. I did find a recording of "Goodbye Pork Pie Hat," which he made with a sextet including Gerry Mulligan in Montreux in 1975, showed his talent as a bass player.

His career and his music continually evolved as he played with many of the top musicians of each era. He began to attract real national attention as a bassist for Red Norvo's trio with Tal Farlow in 1950-1951. He then moved to New York and began working with several major Jazz performers, including Stan Getz, and Art Tatum.

He was the bassist in the famous 1953 Massey Hall concert in Toronto with Charlie Parker, Dizzy Gillespie, Bud Powell, and Max Roach.

He briefly joined his idol, Duke Ellington. His stay with Ellington, however, was brief. Only a few weeks after he joined the band, Mingus had an altercation with Puerto-Rican valve-trombonist Juan Tizol that led to his dismissal. The are several versions of the story. Band member Clarke Terry agrees with Mingus that Tizol did indeed have a knife. It was a switchblade, or as Terry calls it, a "Cuban frog sticker."

There is a delightful article called "The Eloquent Firing of Charles Mingus by Duke Ellington" which has the Mingus and Tizol version of the event, together with the words of Ellington. Mingus had the doubtful honour of being the only band member that Ellington fired personally.

"Mingus Ah Um" is Charles Mingus' most popular album and includes compositions, which are tributes to musicians he admired. Obviously, it included Duke Ellington, but was a little surprised to see Jelly Roll Morton The Penguin Guide to Jazz [190]calls it "*an extended tribute to ancestors.*" Morton kept most of his accolades for himself.

Even after listening to a lot of Charles Mingus' music, I confess I understand neither the man nor his music, I am not sure that he really understood himself either, but he has undoubtedly made an incomparable and intriguing contribution to the world of Jazz.

Philadelphia native **Christian McBride** [Born 1972] is one of the foremost Jazz bassists of his generation. McBride was championed by Benny Carter and his longtime idol and mentor Ray Brown.

McBride would often accompany his father, also a bass player, to gigs, and it was during one of those times that he saw legends Dizzy Gillespie, Dexter Gordon, and Ella Fitzgerald. The shows had a lasting impact on McBride.

He attended the Philadelphia High School for the Creative and Performing Arts, where he rubbed shoulders with classmates like keyboardist **Joey DeFrancesco**, and guitarist Kurt Rosenwinkel. In 1989, he moved to New York City to attend the Juilliard School in Manhattan but left after a year to play professionally. He was eighteen.

So, for over 30 years gigs and albums have flowed from McBride. In 1994, McBride made his debut as leader with "Gettin' to It" with pianist Cyrus Chestnut. Number Two Express followed a year later and featured saxophonist Kenny Garrett, pianist Chick Corea, and drummer Jack DeJohnette, among others.

One of the things that impresses me most about Christian McBride is that he enjoys being a sideman and has recorded over three hundred albums.

McBride closed out the decade with A Family Affair, in which he played the electric bass and reconnected with his R&B roots. He is also an astoundingly gifted electric bassist, and that '70s-vintage funk and soul are every bit as close to his heart as '50s and '60s hard bop.

In 2011, the bassist introduced his big band with The Good Feeling on Mack Avenue. The album, which featured vocals by McBride's wife, singer Melissa Walker, took home the Grammy for Best Large Jazz Ensemble Album.

In February 2020, McBride released his ambitious large-ensemble work The Movement Revisited: A Musical Portrait of Four Icons, celebrating the lives of famed civil rights leaders Rev. Dr. Martin Luther King, Jr., Malcolm X, Rosa Parks, and Muhammad Ali.

I have not done justice to Christian McBride. His prolific output covered duets, trios, and big bands, not to mention all his recordings as a sideman. What an amazing man.

Much of the material here is based on Christian McBride's Biography by Matt Collar, published by AllMusic.

Occasional Instruments

"I never have any trouble playing anything I can think of. The trouble is thinking of what to play."[191]
Stan Getz

I couldn't resist including a short section on the **Harp,** partly because it is such an unlikely Jazz instrument, and partly because of the people I want to talk about

One of the pleasures of exploring the history of Jazz is that it is so easy to take a detour from the main path, and go off on a new adventure, following Alice Coltrane and her harp

The tradition of Jazz harp is today in the capable hands of Brandee Younger [Born 1983]. Carrying on and expanding the tradition of pioneering Jazz harpists Dorothy Ashby and Alice Coltrane, Brandee Younger made her debut in 2007 as a graduate student at NYU Saxophonist Ravi Coltrane enlisted the then 23-year-old to participate in the memorial service for his mother Alice.

Alice Coltrane heavily inspires Younger's music. However, Younger has managed to find her own lane which can veer into soul music, Jazz, hip-hop, or R&B at any moment.

The **Cello** is another instrument which is rarely featured in Jazz. Oscar Pettiford, Ray Brown, and Ron Carter all occasionally played the cello.

Matt Brubeck [Born 1961], one of Dave Brubeck' sons is a cellist, bassist, keyboardist, composer, and arranger. He is both a performer of classical and Jazz music. I had an opportunity to see him play in a 9-piece band at York University. Despite his talent, I came away convinced that the cello does not belong in a Jazz band .

Tomeka Reid [Born 1977] described as a "New Jazz Power Source" by the New York Times is confidently showing the Jazz community that the cello does belong.

A cellist and composer " *Tomeka Reid has emerged as one of the most original, versatile, musicians in Chicago's bustling Jazz and improvised music*

Most of her career has been spent in the academic world and classical music, and she has both a Master's degree and a Doctorate. Her interest in Jazz was sparked by **Nicole Mitchell** (born 1967) an American jazz flautist and composer. They have made many recordings together.

I have omitted several instruments, mainly because I feel they have had less influence on Jazz over the years.

I have not talked about the **Violin,** so Stephane Grappelli is not included. Also missing are Jimmy Smith and Joey De Francesco because I excluded the **Hammond Organ**

The **Flute** gets a mention when I talk about Moe Kauffman in the Canadian section, but perhaps the best known Jazz flutist was Roland Kirk

Was **Rahsaan Roland Kirk** [1935 to 1977]] the coolest person who ever lived?" [193]This is the question posed on "Sheep's Clothing." Website. Maybe. He was certainly one of the most eccentric.

Roland Kirk. The Coolest Person that Ever Lived. Tana Yonas [Writer/Producer][194]

Roland Kirk was blind from the age of two. His first instrument was the trumpet but soon switched to the saxophone. In his concerts he played three saxophones simultaneously He was often dismissed as a showman but came to be recognized as a talented musician. He played in Charles Mingus' band, and they became friends.

I first heard Roland Kirk several years after his death. He was a great flute player and his recording of "Serenade to a Cuckoo" was frequently played on Jazz FM, Toronto's 24-hour Jazz Radio station. I was hooked.

"I Talk with the Spirits" is a 1965 album on which Kirk plays only the flute. It contains the first appearance of the song "Serenade to a Cuckoo", later covered by Jethro Tull.

By 1971, Kirk was known as a charismatic and outspoken maverick who was frustrated that Jazz was ignored by the American media. He was passionate about Jazz, or what he preferred to call "Black Classical Music" He established The Jazz and People's Movement (J&PM), which began in 1969 initially as a regular jam session event at the Village Vanguard on Monday nights the J&PM and their army of peaceful whistle-blowing protesters infiltrated Johnny Carson's *The Tonight Show* and brought organized chaos to *The Dick Cavett Show.*

Their next target was even more prestigious, The Ed Sullivan Show. Kirk assembled a band for the occasion including bassist/composer Charles Mingus who, like Kirk, was a vociferous political firebrand No one expected The Ed Sullivan Show to be controversial, but thanks to an infamous performance by Rahsaan Roland Kirk, it proved to be a memorable spectacle. I drew heavily on the article *"How Rahsaan Roland Kirk Shook Up The Ed Sullivan Show"* [195] to visualize the sabotage of his show. You will enjoy the full article in Udiscovermusic[196]

Rahsaan Roland Kirk was the last Jazz musician to appear on *The Ed Sullivan Show*, which ran for only weeks after that performance. J&MP had run out of steam, and Kirk became a lone crusader, continuing to spread the Jazz message via his concerts and albums.

Ladies Lead the Band

As I have worked on this book, I have tried to make sure that female musicians were well represented.

It was easy for the Vocalists and Pianists, but for the rest it more difficult. Nonetheless, there are a few ladies who have made a name for themselves as band leaders. Usually, it was an all-female band, but not always.

I was surprised to learn that **Lil' Hardin Armstrong** [1898 – 1971] was a Band Leader between 1935 and 1938. Although Lil and Louis had separated in 1931, they had a long working relationship, and she persuaded him to be the lead trumpeter in her band.

By the mid-1930s Lil Hardin Armstrong had successfully established her own solo career as singer, pianist, songwriter, and bandleader. She was a dedicated music professional frequently recording, broadcasting, and performing.

Lil Hardin was also very well-educated and attended the Chicago College of Music (BA, 1928), and the New York School of Music (post-graduate, 1930) and deserves almost as important a place in Jazz History as Louis Armstrong.

Blanche Calloway [1902- 1978] was a gifted bandleader and singer and the sister of **Cab Calloway** [1907-1994]. In 1931, she formed a big band, "Blanche Calloway and Her Joy Boys", which included Ben Webster on tenor saxophone, Chick Webb and Cozy Cole on drums. She was the first woman to lead an all-male orchestra and had enormous success in the early 1930s.

"Blanche Calloway sings with plenty of spirit and sass, showing she was in the same league as her better-known brother."[197] Scott Yanow

By the mid-1930s Blanche Calloway struggled to find bookings as her brother's career grew in popularity In the following decades, Blanche went on to become a nightclub manager in Washington, D.C., and a radio-station program director in Miami Beach; meanwhile, her brother would reach the *Billboard* charts in five consecutive decades, from the 1930s through the 1970s.

Female Jazz Bands came into their own during World War II were serving in the Armed Forces

The International Sweethearts of Rhythm was the first, and probably the best- known integrated all-women's band in the United States. During the 1940s the band featured the best female musicians of the day They played swing and Jazz on a national circuit that included the Apollo Theater in New York City. Their career lasted from 1937 to 1949.[198]

If you enjoy nostalgia for an era, you have never known, just watch the International Sweethearts[199]

This seems a good place to discuss the question of discrimination again, this time both race and gender. The original members, all students, who were African American or mixed raced. In 1943, two white women joined the ensemble, making it an interracial band performing in the Deep South.

An interracial band violated both laws and customs in Mississippi and across the South. As a result, the members of the band faced constant harassment from law enforcement agencies. In fact, the band faced scrutiny from both whites and African Americans.

The Sweethearts also gained an international audience when they spent time entertaining African American troops stationed in Europe. Again, note the continued segregation.

Ivy Benson [1913-1993] and Her All-Girl Band was the first lady bandleader I heard. After leaving school at 14, Ivy bought her first saxophone. She would go on to master the clarinet and trombone as well. From then on, music-making became the focus of her life. She first played as part of touring dance bands before moving from her home in Leeds to London in the late 1930s, where she formed her own 20-piece All Girls swing band.

The band was an enormous success for many years. They became the resident band for BBC radio. They had a six-month booking at the Palladium, London's foremost entertainment venue, the world-famous Albert Hall and so many more places.

Their life was like the American bands we talked about earlier. They were asked to entertain the Allied troops in Europe and the Middle East. Perhaps the highlight of the overseas trip was when Field Marshall Montgomery invited them to perform at the 1945 VE Day celebrations in Berlin.[200].

Unfortunately, Ivy Benson kept losing her musicians, as they would leave for the U.S. to marry G.I.s they had met while touring.

After the post-war period, the all-lady bands gave way to the male-dominated Jazz Scene

I do want to talk about two bands that are with us today. They are hugely different, but each with a large following.

The first is the **Maria Schneider** [Born 1960] Orchestra. Maria Schneider formed her first band in 1988. She is a 2019 NEA Jazz Master and multi–Grammy Award winner for her work in classical, Jazz, and even pop with the late David Bowie. Today the eighteen all-male Maria Schneider Orchestra performs worldwide, " *tackling lush and complex works that bring new energy to the Jazz orchestra landscape[201]."*

Maria Schneider's latest recording Data Lords has the theme of artificial intelligence and technology. She explains: "*No one can deny the great impact that the data- hungry digital world has had on our lives. I know that I'm not alone in struggling to find space—to keep connected with my inner world, the natural world, and just the simpler things in life.*"[202] I confess that I find it difficult to "feel the thinking" behind this recording.

I feel much more comfortable listening to Diva, led by Sherrie Maricle,] a great drummer. **Sherrie Maricle** [Born 1963] has been the leader of the all-female big band, The DIVA Jazz Orchestra for 30 years. She sums up her contribution to Jazz as *Create, Inspire, Educate & Entertain[203]*

Maricle has released several CDs with The DIVA Jazz Orchestra, including Live at the Kennedy Center (2012), Live from Jazz at Lincoln Center (2010), and Live from Jazz at Lincoln Center II (2008).

Maricle also teaches Jazz drumming at The New School in New York City and is a faculty member at the Stanford Jazz Workshop.

Sherrie Maricle is also the leader of a five-person group called Play Five. The other members of the group are Tomoko Ohno, piano Noriko Ueda, bass, Jami Dauber, trumpet, Janelle Reichman, tenor sax/clarinet. To complete her portfolio, she leads a trio called 3D.

Sherrie Maricle is totally devoted to her music and her audience and has been kind enough to exchange emails with me as part of my research. Above all Diva is a delight to watch. They enjoy their playing and really get their audience caught up in the spirit of the music.

This is how Jazz should be played.

Part Four. The Vocalists

Music is as close to God as I know.
Nina Simone[204]

The Ladies of Jazz

The role of female Jazz vocalists goes back to the 1920s, but its role changed over the years.

The first great female vocalist was **Bessie Smith** [1894 – 1937]. The Blues dates to the 19th Century and **W.C. Handy** [1873-1958] was called the Father of the Blues and helped make it popular. But the Blues reached their peak in the 1920s when Bessie Smith burst onto the music scene. She was a big, impressive woman, and had one of the most beautiful voices ever heard on the Jazz scene.

Bessie's career was no more than about six or seven years as with the arrival of the Great Depression the Blues lost its popularity, but its influence lasted for decades.

The 1930s saw the arrival of a new genre of Jazz: Swing. Swing was largely played by big bands and was primarily white music. Swing was essentially dance music, but most bands introduced a female singer into the show. They were not really part of the band; they would just sing one chorus as part of the entertainment.

Duke Ellington called Ivie Anderson his "good luck charm." The "Liltin' Miss Martha Tilton" was the "Sweetheart of Swing."

Helen Ward was an NBC staff singer when Benny Goodman hired her for his weekly *Let's Dance* radio show. In 1935, Helen left the Goodman Orchestra to get married, but she returned for periodic engagements on radio and in motion pictures during the next few years.

Helen Humes gained fame during four years with Count Basie. Some called her the greatest 'Helen' of all the singers of swing. But she was never far from the suggestive, bluesy songs that began her career.[205]

But changes began to happen and when Helen Forrest joined the Harry James band in 1941, she broke new ground for American vocalists. She asked that specific arrangements be written just for her and that the band accompany her as lead vocalist.

This paved the way for Anita O'Day with Stan Kenton and June Christy with Gene Krupa. Both vocalists moved on to success as solo artists.

Billie Holiday was a band singer for many years but went on to have a wonderful solo career. By now the female Jazz vocalist was as big a name as the bands. The evolution continued with these great performers preferring to sing with a small group rather than a big band.

Billie Holiday and the other four ladies I talk about next distinguished themselves in the recording studio and concert halls for their ability to sing with passion, captivating their audience. Their influence lasted and today female Jazz singers still have a great following.

Few people would argue that **Ella Fitzgerald** [1917- 1996] truly was the "Queen of Jazz". In fact, it was only by a twist of fate that we even got to know her name.

She was due to audition at the Appollo, but learned a popular dance duo named the Edwards Sisters would be the feature act on the same night she was to perform. Worried that she would not be as good as the Edwards Sisters, Ella decided to sing instead.[206] . The rest is history.[207]

In the band that night was saxophonist Benny Carter. Impressed with her natural talent, he began introducing Ella to people who could help launch her career. In the process he and Ella became lifelong friends. Her first professional engagement was when Chick Webb hired her to travel with the band for $12.50 a week.

Off stage, and away from people she knew well, Ella was shy and reserved. She was self-conscious about her appearance, and for a while even doubted the extent of her abilities. On stage, however, Ella was surprised to find she had no fear. She felt at home in the spotlight. She said of herself *"Once up there, I felt the acceptance and love from my audience, I knew I wanted to sing before people the rest of my life.*[208]

As well as Benny Carter, there were to be two other men who played a key role in Ella's life. The first is bass player Ray Brown. While on tour with Dizzy Gillespie's band in 1946, Ella fell in love with Ray. The two were married and adopted a son, whom they named Ray, Jr. Unfortunately, busy work schedules hurt Ray and Ella's marriage. The two divorced in 1952 but remained friends for the rest of their lives.

Ray was working for producer Norman Granz on the "Jazz at the Philharmonic" tour. Norman Granz has been described as the *"greatest non-musician in the history of Jazz*[209]*."* He saw Ella as a potential international star, and he convinced her to sign with him. It was the beginning of a lifelong business relationship and friendship.

It was at Granz's suggestion that Ella recorded with Louis Armstrong. That seems to be a very unlikely partnership, but they had a natural way of recording in perfect unison. Their duets are among the most popular recordings of all time.

But her remarkable success and love of her work gradually affected Ella's health and In September of 1986, Ella underwent quintuple coronary bypass surgery.

By the 1990s, Ella had recorded over two hundred albums. In 1991, she gave her final concert at New York's renowned Carnegie Hall. It was the 26th time she performed there. My favourites include recordings made with Ray Brown, Oscar Peterson [piano] and Herb Ellis [guitar]. and the remarkable duets with Louis Armstrong. Perhaps less well- known are recordings made with guitarist Joe Pass

Finally, her health failed completely, and she died in 1996. Ella was one of the greatest Jazz musicians and a delightful modest woman. Anyone who claims to love Jazz will miss her still.

Much of the content above is based on biography by Universal [210]

Sarah Vaughan [1924 -1990] "The Divine One" grew up with a love of music and performing. Her story is almost a Jazz biography classic model. Her parents were also musicians, and the young Sarah studied the piano and organ and sang as a soloist at Mount Zion Baptist Church.

Like Ella Fitzgerald, winning a talent competition at Harlem's Apollo Theater launched her singing career. She was eighteen.

Billie Eckstine saw her and persuaded Earl Hines to hire her. She later joined Eckstine's own band. At that time Charlie Parker, Dizzy Gillespie Art Blakey, and Miles Davis, were playing with Eckstine, and they introduced Sarah to Bebop. She loved it, and soon launched her solo career.

She had a long and successful solo career, occasionally moving away from Jazz for albums of Brazilian music and Beatles songs. Sarah was highly respected in the industry and had the opportunity to perform with many of the best musicians in Jazz. Her most critically acclaimed album was 'How Long Has This Been Going On?' in which she sang with a group that included Oscar Peterson, Joe Pass, Louie Bellson, and Ray Brown.

Many of Sarah Vaughan's songs were or became standards. My personal favourite is "Misty."

On her death, the tributes poured in. Mel Torme said *"She had the single best vocal instrument of any singer working in the popular field,"*[211] e Quincy Jones, who produced some of her recordings said *"Sarah was the most musical singer America has ever known,"*[212] Sarah herself greatly admired Leontyne Price, the opera singer.

Early in her career, **Billie Holiday** [1915 – 1959], was given the nickname "Lady Day" by her good friend and fellow musician, Lester Young. Throughout her career, Holiday had a strong influence on Jazz and pop vocalists. Holiday's style as a vocalist was revolutionary in its ability to manipulate word phrasing and musical tempos.

Sadly, Billie Holiday was probably as well known for her drug and alcohol abuse than for her music. These addictions led to her premature death at the age of 44.

In a difficult early life, Holiday found comfort in music, singing along to the records of Bessie Smith and Louis Armstrong. She followed her mother to New York City in the late 1920's, and at the age of eighteen, producer John Hammond discovered her while she was performing in a Harlem Jazz club. John Hammond was instrumental in getting

Holiday recording work with an up-and-coming clarinetist and bandleader Benny Goodman.

Holiday toured with the Count Basie Orchestra in 1937. The following year, she worked with Artie Shaw and his orchestra. Holiday broke new ground with Shaw, becoming one of the first female African American vocalists to work with a white orchestra.

Holiday was strong-willed and found herself in the middle of a controversy over the song "Strange Fruit." The song was based on a poem about the lynching of two negroes. The song became part of her repertoire for the next 20 years.

She had a unique voice, and just for interest you may like to listen to her and Ella Fitzgerald 's versions of Cole Porter's "Just one of those things."

Billy Holiday was one of the tragic figures in Jazz history who died too early. It would have been wonderful to enjoy her talent for another twenty years.

Much of the material on Billie Holiday is based on a biography in Biography Newsletter[213]

During the 1950s, **Dinah Washington** 1924 - 1963], Queen of the Blues, was one of "the most popular Black female recording artists of the period," recording popular R&B and Jazz tunes. Her biggest hit came in 1959 when she recorded "What a Difference a Day Makes.". Washington gave herself the name "Queen of the Blues."

Like many fellow Jazz singers Dinah Washington had a background in Gospel Music. Born in Alabama, Ruth Lee Jones grew up in a Baptist family in Chicago, singing and playing the piano in the choir at her local church. At the age of fifteen, she performed in a local amateur competition, won and was soon performing in Chicago's nightclubs.

Her big breakthrough came in 1942 when she was spotted by Joe Glaser, Louis Armstrong's manager and on Glaser's recommendation, she joined Lionel Hampton's band in 1943, taking the name Dinah Washington

She also recorded with small combos as well as big bands. This included an impressive array of musicians, such as Ben Webster, Clifford Brown, Clark Terry, Cannonball Adderley, Jimmy Cobb, Max Roach, Wynton Kelly, and Joe Zawinul.

But the singer's musical gifts were offset by a wild and extravagant personal life. Married seven times, Washington battled weight problems and raced through her profits buying shoes, furs, and cars to lift her spirits. Washington also tried many prescription medications, primarily for dieting and insomnia. A mix of the pills she was taking caused her death at the age of thirty-nine.

Richard Havers in Udiscovermusic talks of her death saying, *"On that day, we lost one of the greatest singers to have graced this earth."* [214]

Legendary performer **Nina** Simone [1933 2003] "High Priestess of Soul", was probably the most versatile of the great singers we have discussed in this section. She sang a mix of Jazz, soul, blues, and folk music in the 1950s and '60s.

Nina Simone took to music at an early age, learning to play piano at the age of three and singing in her church's choir. Simone's musical training over the years emphasized classical repertory with Simone later expressing the desire to have been recognized as the first major African American concert pianist. She studied classical piano at the Juilliard School in New York City. She taught piano and worked as an accompanist for other performers while at Juilliard, but she eventually had to leave school after she ran out of funds.

Performing in night clubs, she turned her interest to Jazz, blues and folk music and released her first album in 1957, scoring a Top 20 hit with the track "I Loves You Porgy". Simone's music defied standard definitions. Her classical training showed through, no matter what genre of song she played. She was often called the "High Priestess of Soul," but she hated that nickname. She didn't like the label of "Jazz singer," either. *"If I had to be called something, it should have been a folk singer because there was more folk and blues than Jazz in my playing,"* [215]she later wrote in her autobiography.

My personal favourite album is "Nina Simone sings the Blues"[216]

Nina Simone led a troubled life and in the 1960s, Nina Simone became known as the voice of the Civil Rights Movement. She wrote "Mississippi Goddam" in response to the 1963 assassination of Medgar Evers and the Birmingham church bombing that killed four young African American girls.

As the 1960s ended, Simone tired of the American music scene and the country's deeply divided racial politics. Having been a neighbour of Malcolm X in New York, she later lived in several different countries, including Liberia, Switzerland, England and Barbados before eventually settling down in the South of France. For years, Simone also struggled with severe mental health issues and her finances.

Touring periodically, Simone maintained an ardent fan base that filled concert halls whenever she performed. In 1998, she appeared in the New York tri-state area. The New York *Times* critic Jon Pareles reviewed the concert, noting that "*there is still power in her voice*" and that the show featured "*a beloved sound, a celebrated personality, and a repertory that magnifies them both.*" [217]

Nina Simone clearly did not have a happy life, but Jon Pareles quote beautifully sums up her wonderful contribution to so many genres of music. *"The gift of music is the magic of the world. It is a discipline that increases understanding. And expresses the spirit of the human being."*[218]

In my opinion **Abbey Lincoln** [1930 – 2010], deserves a place with the four great vocalists I have just discussed, but she never quite reached those heights.

This is what she said at her induction into the National Endowments for the Arts in 1903." *The gift of music is the magic of the world. It is a discipline that increases understanding. And expresses the spirit of the human being. I thank God and my ancestors for the music.*[219]"

Strongly influenced by Jazz icons Billie Holiday and Louis Armstrong, both of whom she met early in her career, Abbey Lincoln's distinctive vocal style, thought-provoking writing, and spirited personality secured her a place among the Jazz greats[220]

She recorded her first album with Jazz great Benny Carter in 1956, She then recorded a series of albums for the Riverside label with drummer

Max Roach. Lincoln's collaborations with Roach (to whom she was married from 1962-70 included the recording, We Insist! Freedom Now Suite in 1960. This was the beginning of a more social and political activist approach to her music.[221]

Over the years, she worked with some of the biggest names in Jazz, including Sonny Rollins, Eric Dolphy, Coleman Hawkins, Miles Davis, and Stan Getz. Abbey Lincoln was an exceptionally talented lady.

You might enjoy hearing her and Max Roach together.[222] In addition to her music, Lincoln also pursued acting, appearing in films, and teaching drama at the California State University.

I often listen to the music of an artist as I write about them. Now I am listening to The Very Best of Abbey Lincoln, a 2 CD collection released in 2020. Every song is sung with heartfelt sincerity and the purity of her voice is musical perfection.

Cassandra Wilson's (born 1955) recording career began in 1986 and, by the time she joined Blue Note, seven years later, in 1993, she had already made eight albums. At Blue Note, though, beginning with her debut, *Blue Light 'Til Dawn*. Udiscovermusic said of her *"she took her music to another level by patenting a piquant marinade of Jazz, blues and folk flavors."*[223]

Uniquely among female Blue Note musicians, this singular style, combined with her trademark vocals allowed Wilson to create a new category of music. As well as being a singer who can make other people's songs sound like her own, Wilson is a more-than-capable songwriter. She picked up her first Grammy for her second Blue Note album, *New Moon Daughter*, in 1995, and gained another with 2009's *"Luverly."* Even though she left the company in 2009, her Blue Note albums are the most impressive in her portfolio.

Jazz or Not?

In his book "The History of Jazz" Ted Gioia raises the question as to whether Dianna Krall and Norah Jones are Jazz singers. They are two of the most commercially successful Jazz-influenced singers. Their music is introspective and sincere, and critics question what genre they belonged to. The paragraph below is about Norah Jones and Blue Note.

Three years into the label's seventh decade, along came an artist who took Blue Note executives by surprise with a record that was both controversial and brilliant[224] – but was it, Jazz? To some, sitar player Ravi Shankar's daughter, Norah Jones, was anything but, yet according to Michael Cuscuna, a record producer: *"I was absolutely thrilled when Blue Note signed Norah Jones. She was a Jazz artist, playing piano and singing standards with an acoustic bass and a Jazz drummer."* [225] , Bruce Lundvall[226], with his whole concern about the integrity of Blue Note, offered to sign her to the Manhattan label, which was more pop oriented. But Norah said, *"No. I want to be on Blue Note. That's who I signed with. I love that label. I grew up with that, and that's where I want to be."*[227]

This proved to be the right decision for both Norah Jones and Blue Note. Jazz is full of events, although small in themselves were career-changing moments.

The same question may be asked of two of the best recordings of all time: "Cry me a River" by **Julie London** [1926 – 2000] and "Fever" by **Peggy Lee** [1920 – 2002]

They are not usually regarded as Jazz singers, although both these ladies' recorded songs with **Barney Kessel** on guitar and **Ray Leatherwood** on bass provided the backing for Julie London and Joe Mondragon on bass and **Shelly Manne** on drums for Peggy Lee.

Ella Fitzgerald was originally meant to debut the song "Cry me a River" as part of the score for the 1955 film *Pete Kelly's Blues*. However, when the song was dropped from the movie, it was Julie London who first recorded it, including it on her debut LP, "Julie Is Her Name."

In 1958, Peggy Lee's cover of "Fever" not only breathed new life into the R&B classic but revitalized her career. While Lee remained a favourite singer among Jazz fans, her swing-era pop vocals had begun to lose relevance among younger audiences. Her subdued yet sensual take on "Fever," however, spoke directly to a younger crowd while bearing all the wit and sophistication of the coolest Jazz records.

The songs I mentioned are two of my favourite recordings, sung by two of my favourite singers. Is it Jazz or not? I don't mind either way. I just listen and enjoy.

The Lasting Impact of the Blues

I recently had the good fortune to watch a program about **Bessie Smith** and a concert by **Jazzmeia Horn**, one of today's best Jazz vocalists on the same evening. It allowed me to think about the evolution of Jazz singing over one hundred years.

The first thing that needs to be said is that they are both products of their time and upbringing. Bessie Smith was born in Tennessee, was orphaned before she was ten and grew up in a poor part of Chicago whereas Jazzmeia grew up in comfortable Baptist Church surroundings in Texas.

Bessie Smith was called the "Empress of the Blues" and when I listen to Bessie Smith what I hear is raw power and emotion. This is described in a beautifully written essay by Clare Tompkins for NPR [National Public Radio]

"She sang about the kind of trouble that most people knew well, and her shouts and lamentations identified a depth of feeling that nearly everyone experiences but would be hard-pressed to describe."*[228]*

But where did that come from? In the early days in Chicago, Bessie was close to starvation but made a little money for her siblings by singing in churches and on the streets. At the age of sixteen she met Ma Raney and joined her on tour. By the age of twenty-four she was out on her own and became the highest paid Black musician in the USA. Understanding a bit about the personal and historical background helps us understand songs like "Gimme a pig foot and a bottle of beer"

Jazzmeia Horn had quite a different background. Her life was a much more comfortable than Bessie's and her education led her towards a career in Jazz. Her first idol was Sarah Vaughan. She became obsessed with Sarah until she realized that she was copying Sarah Vaughan rather than learning from her. She was also a great admirer of Ella Fitzgerald and is a great scat singer. There is an excellent video by Jazzmeia describing Ella's style, [229]and including beautiful scat singing on Blue Skies[230].Her style is smooth compared with Bessie's rough and the songs are more complex and sophisticated, but they are still deeply personal.

Can you trace the route from 1920 to 2020? I think so. You may not hear Bessie Smith directly in today's music, but the Blues, together with Ragtime was the foundation of Jazz we know it, and its presence has never gone away.

Mahalia Jackson, [1911-1972] who was primarily a Gospel singer recognized the influence of Bessie Smith. Maybe Mahalia's gospel background influenced her blues.

Her influence extended further. You can hear that if you listen to **Aretha Franklin's** "I Never Loved a Man the Way I Love You" It was recorded in 1967. What an amazing Blues singer Aretha Franklin was.

Female vocalists are enjoying immense success, and I can see the emotion, the influence of their world reflected in their compositions and a love of performing.

In passing I highly recommend a recent movie with Ma Rainey[231], a friend and rival to Bessie, being played by Viola Davis. Not only is it a very entertaining movie, but it also adds greatly to our understanding of the blues era.

The Gentlemen

I am not a great fan of male Jazz singers, and there are only five on my list. I did not include Frank Sinatra, Bing Crosby, Dean Martin, Tony Bennett, and Nat King Cole. I liked them all, and they recorded songs that could be classified as Jazz, but I do not consider them Jazz Vocalists.

We should also remember that for most of the lifetime of Jazz, the men were the musicians, and the role of the ladies was to sing.

The earliest Jazz singer I enjoyed was **George Melly** [1926 – 2007], back in my early days of listening to Jazz in England.

People, probably including me, remember George Melly for his eccentric personality as much as his music. His obituary in the Daily Telegraph[232] is the closest I have found to summing up this amazing man.

"George Melly, the Jazz singer, author and raconteur, leched, drank and blasphemed his way around the clubs and pubs of the British Isles and provided pleasure to the public for five decades"[233].

Appearing in the 1950s with Mick Mulligan's Magnolia band and later for nearly three decades with John Chilton's Footwarmers, Melly followed a well-established routine of singing numbers from the 1920's. His foremost influence were Bessie Smith, Fats Waller and Jelly Roll Morton interspersed with bawdy anecdotes."

He described himself on one occasion as "Bessie Smith in a Tweed Suit"[234]

A Jazz Singer with a vastly different style was **Joe Williams** [1911-1999]. From the beginning, it was Williams' ability, to make blues out of ballads and ballads out of blues that made him a favourite in both Jazz clubs and supper clubs; with small combos and big bands, in Carnegie Hall, the <u>Monterey</u> Jazz Festival and every saloon, concert stage and Jazz event in between.

Williams had sung with some of the big names during the first 15 years of his career including Lionel Hampton, Coleman Hawkins, Harry "Sweets" Edison, George Shearing and Cannonball Adderley, but it was his seven years (1954-61) with Count Basie that catapulted him into a solo singing star. It was the Basie years I remember him for, and I still enjoy his singing.

As I have read more about my favourite musicians, it has struck me that the Jazz World is exceedingly small. As far as I know, Joe Williams never played with George Shearing, but they were close friends.

Some may disagree, but I remember **Mel Torme** [1925-1999] as a Jazz artist, although his very wide repertoire made him a favourite of a much wider audience.

He was nicknamed "The Velvet Fog" due to his smooth vocal style. Tormé composed the music for "The Christmas Song" (also known as "Chestnuts Roasting on an Open Fire") and co-wrote the lyrics with Bob Wells. He won two Grammy Awards and was nominated 14 times.

In 1942, he joined a band led by Chico Marx of the Marx Brothers as a singer, drummer, and arranger. Tormé made his movie debut in Frank Sinatra's first film, "Higher and Higher," in 1943. He gained popularity as a solo singer with hits like "Careless Hands".

Mel Tormé was known for his Jazz-oriented pop singing style and worked steadily from the 1940s to the 1990s. He had a versatile career that spanned nightclubs, concert halls, radio, television, movies, and music. Tormé's contributions to Jazz music were significant. He formed the vocal quintet Mel Tormé and His Mel-Tones in 1944, which had several hits fronting Artie Shaw's band and on their own. The Mel-Tones were among the first Jazz-influenced vocal groups.

Gregory Porter [Born 1971], His deep, golden voice saw him achieve a rapid rise to success in his early forties and he is the most famous male Jazz singer today[235].

Despite a lifetime of singing, it was two releases on American label Motema label in the early 2010's which brought him to critical acclaim and being signed by Universal Records, part of Blue Note.'

His first album for Blue Note," Liquid Spirit" won Best Jazz Vocal at the 2014 Grammy Awards and achieved huge mainstream acclaim and pop chart success internationally.

Gregory Porter has touted extensively in the years since, winning over bigger and bigger audiences with his soulful compositions and sensitive, blues-infused treatment of ballads.

Kurt Elling [Born 1967] The Guardian described Chicago-born Kurt Elling as *"a kind of Sinatra with superpowers."*[236]

With 10 Grammy nominations under his belt, his technical skill and flexibility is combined with the spirit of a true entertainer.

Elling was hailed by The New York Times as *"the standout male Jazz vocalist of our time"* and is just at ease performing classic songs as he is with vocalese, scat singing and modern Jazz stylings.

For a great insight into his mix of entertainment with high-level Jazz. You should listen to his tongue-in-cheek version of "Pennies from Heaven."

Part Five. My Canadian Years

Playing Jazz is like painting with sound."
Oscar Peterson[237]

I need to include a caveat here. At the time of writing [September 2023] it is not clear what is going to happen to Jazz in Canada. During the COVID pandemic all the Jazz clubs in Toronto closed. Some have reopened and new ones have opened. Some of the familiar names have come to the stage again, and there are new names appearing. This is very encouraging, but I don't know yet who are the stars of the future.

What is encouraging is that International Jazz musicians have begun to recognize that there is still an audience for Jazz. Amongst the visitors to Toronto have been Herbie Hancock, Hiromi, and Samara Joy.

By the time I moved to Canada in 1985, interest in Jazz was past its peak. In the 1960s and 1970s Toronto, Montreal and Vancouver had many Jazz Clubs, and the big bands had not faded as early as in the USA. I remember reading an interview with Rob McConnell, saying that he would have as many as ten gigs a week.

The Colonial was one of the most famous Jazz venues in Canada from the 1950s until it closed in the late '70s. The venue hosted Jazz legends including Oscar Peterson, Ella Fitzgerald, Billie Holiday, Dizzy Gillespie, Miles Davis, Carmen McRae, Duke Ellington, Benny Goodman, Thelonious Monk, Art Blakey, and Jimmy Smith. Sadly, Canada today sees very few of the top American Jazz musicians.

I want to talk a bit about Jazz in Canada before the 1980's, but the focus will be mainly on some of the great musicians that Canada has produced; many of whom I have had the pleasure of seeing and meeting.

The Greatest Jazz Concert Ever

Any article about Jazz in Canada must include one of the greatest Jazz events in Canadian history, if not the complete history of Jazz.

On May 15, 1953, alto saxophonist Charlie Parker, trumpeter Dizzy Gillespie, pianist Bud Powell, bassist Charlie Mingus and drummer Max Roach stepped onto the stage of Massey Hall and played a concert that would assume mythic proportions. And this was the one and only time that they ever played together.

The event inspired the writing of two books and numerous newspaper and magazine articles. and record covers, and many declared it "The Greatest Jazz Concert Ever." Was it the greatest concert? The jury is probably out on that. Certainly, it was disliked by some people as Bebop really had not caught on, and the group seemed to have little cohesion, either personally or musically. The recording of the concert has been listed as the fourth bestselling Jazz Album[238]. of all time, behind: Kind of Blue [Miles Davis], A Love Supreme [John Coltrane] and Time Out [Dave Brubeck

I have a copy of the recording, more because I feel it ought to be in my collection than because I enjoy listening to it.

Unfortunately, Massey Hall was not full because people had opted to watch the boxing match between Rocky Marciano and Jersey Joe Walcott on TV. Ironically, the fight lasted less than one round. I hope that night really wasn't the greatest night in Canada's Jazz history.

McConnell and Nimmons – Giants of Jazz

Rob McConnell and Phil Nimmons were both leaders of big bands, probably the best Canada has produced.

Rob McConnell [1935-2010] was a Canadian Jazz trombonist, composer, and arranger. He is best known for establishing and leading the big band The Boss Brass, which he directed from 1967 to 1999. He began his performing career in the early 1950s, performing and studying with Clifford Brown, Don Thompson, and later with Canadian trumpeter and bandleader. Guy Lombardo.

In 1968, he formed The Boss Brass, a big band that was to last until the 1990s. The instrumentation of the band was originally sixteen pieces, consisting of trumpets, trombones, French horns, and a rhythm section but no saxophones. He introduced a saxophone section in 1970 and expanded the trumpet section to include the fifth trumpet in 1976, bringing the total to twenty-two members.

In 1977, McConnell recorded a double LP called Big Band Jazz. On McConnell's direct cut double LP, recording, an entire side (15 minutes and 2 seconds) was devoted to a version of Gershwin's "Porgy and Bess". The double album won the Juno Award for Best Jazz Album in 1978

In 1997, he was inducted into the Canadian Music Hall of Fame, and in 1998 was made an Officer of the Order of Canada. McConnell and Boss Brass made an incomparable contribution to Jazz in Canada.

Many well-known musicians started their careers with Boss Brass, including Ed Bickert, Guido Basso, Moe Koffman, Terry Clarke, John Johnson, Mike Murley and more.

Phil Nimmons [Born 1923]. is often referred to as the "Dean of Canadian Jazz," and is known for his work as a clarinetist, bandleader, composer, arranger, and educator. After attending the Julliard School and the Royal Conservatory of Music, he formed his own bands, most notably the popular group Nimmons 'N' Nine and later Nimmons 'N' Nine Plus Six.

A founding member of the Canadian League of Composers, he also co-founded the Advanced School of Contemporary Music with Oscar Peterson and Ray Brown. Phil had a major influence on establishing Jazz programs across Canada, and taught at the University of Toronto, Jazz Studies program for over 45 years.

Phil was awarded the inaugural JUNO Award for best Jazz album in 1977. In 2002, he received Canada's highest honour for an artist, the Governor General's Performing Arts Award for Lifetime Artistic Achievement.

I enjoy this comment by Phil Nimmons, *"I've always been the Jazzer,"* he told Jazz journalist, Mark Miller *"I'm still going through the process of trying to convince my friends that this is music, too.[239]"* Nimmons 1987

I need to make one more change before I submit my final manuscript. Phil Nimmons died yesterday, April 10th, 2024, He was one hundred years old. His influence on Jazz Music and Jazz Musicians in Canada will never be forgotten.

1923, the year of his birth, Bessie Smith, and the King Oliver Band, with Louis Armstrong, made their first recordings. Phil Nimmons lived through an amazing century of Jazz.

Three Gentlemen of Jazz

Oliver Jones [Piano], Norman Marshall Villeneuve and [Drums] Dave Young [Bass].

One of my most treasured albums is "Just in Time" which these gentlemen recorded together in 1999. As Canadians, they had met but had never recorded together before. The result was a magnificent album, which, in my opinion, matched the greatness of The Oscar Peterson trio.

Let me tell you a bit about these gentlemen, and where they fit into the Canadian Jazz scene.

Oliver Jones [Born 1934] is second only to Oscar Peterson as a Canadian Jazz pianist. Oliver's musical training was entirely in the classical realm. He studied music with Oscar Peterson's sister, Daisy Peterson Sweeny. Both Oscar and Oliver developed a solid foundation of musical knowledge and technique as pupils of Oscar's sister.

I am not going to take you through Oliver Jones' long and illustrious career, but rather try to give you a feel for the man he was.

He spent many years in Puerto Rico before coming back to Montreal with a real drive to become a Jazz Musician and travelled around the world. Jones never enjoyed the kind of international fame that Peterson had in his life. That didn't matter. He was so proud of the respect and the honours he received, and the joy of having people listen to him.

Jones retired in 2000, but in 2004 he and Oscar Peterson were asked to play at the 25th Anniversary of the Montreal Jazz Festival. Oliver said that *"even though Oscar and I had been good friends since we grew up together, we had never performed together"*[240]

Oliver agreed to come out of retirement and perform the concert with his old friend and mentor. NPR said, *"YouTube has what is arguably the best 6 minutes and 49 seconds you'll ever spend in front of a computer screen".*[241]

Absolutely. Wonderful music beautifully recorded. I hope that one day someone will pay tribute to YouTube and the amazing contribution it has made to Jazz music.

Award winner, band leader, recording artist and Jazz master, drummer **Norman Marshall Villeneuve** [Born 1938] is an iconic and much-loved figure in Canadian Jazz history.

Norm was born in Montreal and grew up in the Little Burgundy area, home to Oscar Peterson and Oliver Jones. Like Oliver Jones, who is his cousin, he studied piano with Daisy Peterson,

Oscar's sister. Daisy Peterson [1920 – 1913 although a teacher of classical music, deserves a special place in Canadian Jazz history.

With a natural talent for rhythm and a love for Jazz, Norm, at the age of 8, began to teach himself how to play drums, avidly studying Jazz legends including Art Blakey, to whom Norm has dedicated his life's work. In his career, has worked with a legion of Jazz greats, including Duke Ellington.

In 1974 Norm moved from Montreal to Toronto and quickly established himself in the Jazz clubs around town, and later took his Norman Marshall Villeneuve Jazz Message[242] Sextet on a successful cross-Canada tour. In 2013 Norm returned to his beloved Montreal where he continues his life's work.

Norman Marshall Villeneuve has developed and given innumerable performance opportunities to new generations of those who now comprise the best of Canadian Jazz, from established musicians, including Robi Botos, Mike Downes, Bob Brough, Artie Roth and Meirion Kelly, whom I will talk more about shortly, to college graduates, and, to new Canadians.

The notes above are based on an article from Soul Tone Cymbals[243]

I was lucky enough to meet Norm on several occasions in Toronto. His caring for the next generation, or perhaps the generation after next, was shown by inviting young players to join him at gigs. My son Aaron played with him several times. I recall watching him one night at Chalker's Jazz Club. He made no concession to the three young members of the band; it was their challenge to keep up with his drive.

I just loved watching him. He played with incredible enthusiasm and energy, and every performance was a tribute to Art Blakey.

126

Dave Young [Born 1940] is an Order of Canada recipient, a Juno Award-winner and a respected bassist, composer, arranger, and educator. He has performed on Canadian and international stages for over five decades playing both Jazz and classical music. Young has collaborated with Peter Appleyard, Guido Basso, Oliver Jones, Lenny Breau and Molly Johnson, among countless others. Young also played with Oscar Peterson for decades.

I enjoyed watching him play. Added enjoyment was when during the intermissions he would walk round chatting to the audience. He had the most entertaining reminiscences of his travels with Oscar Peterson,

On his tribute to Oscar "Aspects of Oscar," Young's quintet includes Kevin Turcotte (trumpet), Robi Botos (piano), Reg Schwager (guitar), and Terry Clarke (drums). Together they perform some of Peterson's most-loved originals and arrangements of Jazz standards.

Fellow musicians admire Dave Young as much as he is loved by his audiences, and until recently he was a popular lecturer in the Music Faculty of the University of Toronto. *"To my way of thinking, Dave Young is one of the most talented bassists on the Jazz scene. His harmonic simpatico and unerring sense of time, have kept him in the foreground of the Jazz picture."* -Renee Rosnes, Artistic Director[244]

Some Very Talented Canadian Jazz Musicians

Let me start with **Archie Alleyne** [1933-2013]. He is truly one of the great names of Canadian Jazz.

When Billie Holiday performed in Toronto, she knew who she wanted to provide the beat beneath her voice: Archie Alleyne the drummer of choice for touring Jazz greats. During his lengthy career, the pioneering musician not only helped to break down colour barriers in the city – becoming the first black performer to take the stage in many whites-only venues – but also mentored young Black musicians and spoke up publicly on their behalf.[245]

People may debate whether Archie Alleyne or Norman Villeneuve was the best drummer Canada ever produced. It really doesn't matter; they both made a major impact in the Jazz community and in encouraging young people to develop their talents. For that reason. I am going to focus as much on the man, as his music.

Young Archie's formative years were spent in the busy Kensington Market, at the time a crowded Jewish area that was also home to the city's small Black community. On the Sabbath, Archie would earn a dime here and there, doing work that his Jewish neighbours were prohibited from performing on that day for religious reasons.

The self-education of one of the best hard-bop drummers in Canada had begun, though he never learned to read music. "*When Archie got into the drums, that's all he wanted to do,*" [246]his friend Richard. Blackman recalled. "*Drumming was his whole life*"

As opportunities began to emerge for Alleyne, so too, did racial obstacles. Black musicians were routinely denied rehearsal space by white landlords. Most Jazz venues were closed to Black audiences.

In 1967, Alleyne was severely injured in a car accident. After lengthy rehabilitation, he resumed performing but his heart was no longer in Jazz. In 1969, he shifted away from music, becoming a partner in a new restaurant, the Underground Railroad. It was not until 1982, and the drummer returned to his first love, Jazz

A six-week tour of African cities in 1989 with the Oliver Jones Trio galvanized his desire to educate young Canadians about the African roots of Jazz and contemporary music such as hip-hop. Within a year of his return to Canada, he had started the Evolution of Jazz Ensemble to give young people what he had lacked as a budding musician: rehearsal and performance opportunities.

"*He never forgot his own struggles or those of his parents,*" his long-time partner , Elvira Fernandes said "*He believed if he let people know the contribution others had made advancing the cause, then his struggles would have been worth it.*"[247]

It is impossible to talk about Archie Alleyne without mentioning **Kollage,** one of the best bands in Canada for many years.

The award-winning "hard bop" sextet Kollage was originally formed in 1999, as Archie Alleyne joined forces with Doug Richardson [1937 - 2016], a well-known saxophonist, to create a band that would preserve the tradition and importance of Jazz born of the Blue Note Records era of the '50s and '60s.

Since then, Kollage has been one of Canada's most influential Jazz bands, with alumni that includes some of Canada's best known Jazz musicians, including Robi Botos, piano, Alexis Baro, trumpet, and Artie Roth, bass.

One of the original members was Mei Kelly, a talented trombonist. I first met him when he was the Jazz teacher of my two sons, and he really encouraged them to play Jazz music. Mei also introduced them to Archie Alleyne, who gave them the opportunity to join The Evolution of Jazz Ensemble. The Jazz world seems to be a remarkably close community at times. Mei has made recordings with Norman Villeneuve Marshall, my favourite being "Caravan"

Oscar Peterson and Ed Bickert have been covered in the Musicians section and represent the best in Canadian Jazz. Other musicians who have made a major impact on Canadian Jazz. Many of them got their start with either Rob McConnell or Phil Nimmons.

Moe Koffman [1928-2001] was one of the few Canadian musicians I had heard in England. Others I remember well; Joni Mitchell and Buffy Ste Marie, but they belonged to different genres.

Moe Koffman spent the early 1950s in the USA and on his return to Canada in 1956 he became the booking agent for George's Spaghetti House[248] in 1956 (remaining in this capacity and appearing there roughly one week each month with his band, until 1994)[249]

"Swinging Shepherd Blues," written and recorded by Moe Koffman in 1958 was a worldwide hit, and helped not only Koffman himself, but also the flute as a Jazz instrument. Koffman told The Montreal Gazette in 1973, *"It wasn't meant to be a hit parade song, and nobody expected it to be....* *Jazz people would like it and Jazz stations might play it. But that was all.* [250]"Because of the worldwide success of "Swinging Shepperd Blues" much of Koffman's music has been overlooked. I n all he recorded thirty albums over his 40-year career.

Guido Basso [1937-2023] died last year, and a tribute from fellow musician, Chase Sanborn, sums up the man and his music.

"When Guido Basso played the flugelhorn, he spoke in a way that was as warm and beautiful as he was a person. I doubt there is anyone who ever met him, even in passing, who was not touched by his grace, and when you hear him play a ballad, you know."[251]

Basso was born in Montreal, but by the 1960s he had moved to Toronto and in 1968 became one of the founders of Rob McConnell and the Boss Brass, with whom he played for many years.

Seeing him, not so many years ago, I can attest to the beauty of his music. In the various tributes, he was described as a mentor, who loved to help develop the talents of younger musicians.

Don Thompson [Born 1940] is another veteran of the Canadian Jazz scene. Thompson is an amazingly versatile musician who plays double bass, piano, and vibes. The roles he played were as varied. Thompson's career as a performer, recording artist, producer, session musician, and music educator has lasted for more than 50 years.

Thompson was a member of the Boss Brass (bassist 1969-82 and pianist in 1988), throughout his career his versatility provided him with very varied opportunities.

He was Moe Koffman's bassist from 1970 to 1974 and pianist from 1975 to 1978). He also played bass and even drums for Lenny Breau.

He maintained a lengthy association with the guitarist Ed Bickert, probably the greatest Canadian Jazz guitarist, in various Jazz settings.

He was also in demand in the USA and Europe and from 1982-7 was a concert partner with George Shearing. He was also an accompanist to the singer Mel Tormé.

I cannot think of a better way of ending this profile than by hearing what Thompson has to say about being a multi-instrument musician.

"I hear a musical sound, a melody, in my head, but as soon as I touch the bass, I realize the limitations of the instrument. I can play stuff on the piano in my sleep that I can't come close to on the vibes, and the bass is so much harder than either one of them, that to play anything at all on it is a miracle."[252]

Listening to musicians like Don Thompson, I realized just how deep their love is for Jazz music. They no longer play with the big names in the USA. But they still play, albeit for smaller audiences. As Jazz fans we are fortunate that these wonderful musicians still enjoy playing.

Pat Labarbera [Born 1944., saxophonist, flutist, clarinetist, composer, and Jazz educator spent the first thirty years of his life in the United States before moving to Toronto in 1974. He studied at the Berklee College of Music, and soon after graduating, began to make his presence felt with the best of the American big bands.

He has collaborated with the biggest entertainers in the business including Frank Sinatra, Tony Bennett, Dizzy Gillespie, Ella Fitzgerald, Chick Corea, Woody Shaw, and McCoy Tyner.

Pat LaBarbera has been among the key members of the Toronto Jazz scene for the past three-plus decades, claiming Junos for writing and performing with his own Jazz ensembles all along the way. Like other top musicians, Labarbera has given back to the industry, and has been on the teaching faculty at Humber College for the past several years instructing on Saxophone,

His album, Deep in a Dream, won the 2000 Juno Award for Best Mainstream Jazz Album. In 2013, Pat and pianist Don Thompson released A Little Simple Magic, a duo recording featuring twelve standards.

Peter Appleyard [1928-2013] was born in England where he played drums in various dance bands and the RAF band. He moved initially to Bermuda and then to Canada in the 1950s. It was not until then that he started playing the vibraphone.

Appleyard travelled all round the world and played with a variety of musicians including Mel Torme. But one of the highlights of his career was playing with the Benny Goodman sextet in the 1970s, where he succeeded Lionel Hampton.

Of Appleyard's vibraphone playing, Jack Batten[253] *"He's most reminiscent of Red Norvo in style, given the impeccable taste and the easy rhythmic lift he displays as he glides over his vibes."*

I talk a little more about Peter Appleyard later and his album "Sophisticated Ladies" on which he accompanies top Canadian Lady vocalists.

Doug Riley:[1945 -2007] was a Canadian pianist, composer, and producer, who was also known as Dr. Music. He studied piano at the Royal Conservatory of Music and music at the University of Toronto. He played with various bands and artists, such as the Silhouettes, Ray Charles, Moe Koffman, Anne Murray, Gordon Lightfoot, and Molly Johnson, to name but a few.

He also participated in over three hundred album projects in different genres. He is remembered as one of the most influential and versatile musicians in Canada's history. He was greatly respected and admired by his fellow musicians.

Guido Basso said of him *"He was respected worldwide and his easygoing warm nature and 'light up a room' smiles are still sorely missed and fondly remembered by any who were fortunate enough to call him their friend."*[254]

You will have seen from the profiles above that Canada has a rich tradition of developing highly talented musicians. We have benefitted enormously from these musicians continuing to perform into their eighties.

I hope their successors give us as much pleasure. Here is one who is.

Robi Botos [Born 1978] is undoubtedly the best Jazz pianist in Canada. He and his family came to Canada from Hungary in 1998. and made an immediate impact on the Toronto scene.

He was Oscar Peterson's last protegee and has played many tributes to his mentor. From the hard-bop style of Bill Evans and Herbie Hancock to the swing of Oscar Peterson and the heartfelt melodic expression of Mulgrew Miller and Cedar Walton, Robi has managed to master the technique of his idols, all the while displaying his musical expressions in a voice that is purely his own. He always incorporates an element of the music he grew up listening to.[255]

He is often accompanied by his brother Frank on drums. Frank's son, Norbert, is also a drummer. I first saw him as a young teenager, with enormous talent. Now in his mid-20s, he is greatly in demand, playing with musicians like Mark Eisenman and Neil Swainson.

Canadian Ladies of Jazz

Jane Bunnett [Born 1956] is a Canadian musician and educator who plays the soprano saxophone, flute, and piano. As well as having a successful career, she is known for performing Afro-Cuban Jazz and collaborating with Cuban musicians.

Mary Jane Bunnett originally studied classical piano at the Royal Conservatory of Music, but tendonitis cut short that career path. After seeing the Charles Mingus group perform in San Francisco, she was inspired to play advanced Jazz. The influence of saxophonist Steve Lacy, with whom she studied in Paris, is evident in her work on the soprano saxophone, while her flute playing is rooted in classical study in Canada.

She has won awards and honours for her music, including five Juno Awards and an appointment as an Officer of the Order of Canada. She also leads an all-female Afro-Cuban/Jazz group called Maqueque, which has released four albums so far.

Born in Vancouver, British Columbia, **Ingrid Jensen** [Born 1966] is one of the most gifted trumpeters of her generation. After graduating from Berklee College of Music in 1989, she went on to record three highly acclaimed CDs, soon becoming one of the most in-demand trumpet players on the jazz scene.

Ingrid settled in New York City in the mid-1990s where she joined the jazz orchestra of Maria Schneider (1994-2012}. More recently, Ingrid has performed with Terri-Lyne Carrington and her Mosaic Project, and the all-star ensemble, Artemis.

She is a featured soloist on the Christine Jensen Jazz Orchestra's Juno-award-winning album, Treelines (2011), and its successor, Habitat (2013] One of her most frequent and closest collaborators is her sister, saxophonist, and composer Christine Jensen

She has also performed alongside Corrine Bailey Rae on *Saturday Night Live* and recorded with Canadian pop icon Sarah McLachlan.

Jensen is a dedicated jazz educator, having taught trumpet at the University of Michigan, she is currently Dean of Jazz Arts at Manhattan School of Music.

Brandi Disterheft [Born 1980] is a Canadian jazz bassist, singer and composer who was born in Vancouver, British Columbia. She has won a Juno Award for her debut album in 2008 and has performed in various countries and venues, including Carnegie Hall. She is known for her fiery bass playing and her innovative live shows, where she sings in both English and French.

She has also collaborated with legendary pianists such as Oscar Peterson, Hank Jones and Oliver Jones. Her latest album, Surfboard, features saxophonist George Coleman and was released in 2020.

Unfortunately, like many Canadian musicians, she now lives and plays in New York.

Latin Jazz in Toronto

There is much Latin Jazz in Toronto. Toronto has a Jazz scene that is vibrant and thriving, and it supports a variety of genres and styles, including Latin Jazz and world music. You can find bars and clubs where you can enjoy live Latin Jazz performances, such as: Lula Lounge, Reservoir Lounge

If you want to listen to some Latin Jazz on the radio, you can tune in to "Café Latino" on JAZZ.FM91 It explores the best Latin Jazz from all over the world, including Brazilian and Afro-Cuban music and Latin Jazz from the U.S., Venezuela, Spain and, of course, Canada.

There are many talented Latin Jazz musicians in Toronto. Some of the best-known ones are:

Amanda Martinez [Born 1992]. She is a singer-songwriter who blends Latin, Jazz, and folk music in her songs. She has performed at various festivals and venues around the world, including the Pan American Games, the Blue Note Jazz Festival, and the Glenn Gould Studio. She is also the host of the JazzFM91 Latin program.

Hilario Duran [Born 1953]. He is a pianist, composer, and arranger who has been called one of the greatest Cuban Jazz musicians of all time. He has collaborated with renowned artists, such as Chucho Valdes and Jane Bunnett. He has also won several awards, including three Juno Awards, two Grammy nominations, and an Order of Canada.

He and Jane Bunnett have worked together for a long time, promoting Latin music, and bringing Latin musicians to Canada

Alexis Baro [Born 1977] was born into a musical family in Havana, Cuba. Classically trained, he took up the trumpet at the age of eight and completed his musical education at the prestigious Amadeo Roldán Music Conservatory in Havana.

After moving to Toronto, Canada in 2001, Canadian jazz drummer Archie Alleyne discovered him, where he flourished as a writer and performer for eight years as a member of Kollage.

As a band member, he was nominated for "Best Jazz Trumpeter" by the Canadian National Jazz Awards in the years 2006, 2007, and 2008. Baro has participated in more than eighty albums and can be heard as a featured soloist. Highlights in his solo career include the opening for Herbie Hancock. He has released six albums as a soloist including" "Sandstorm". which was nominated for a Juno Award in 2018.

Canadian Vocalists

I have not included any male Canadian vocalists. People might argue for the inclusion of Matt Bublé, but Ted Gioia expresses views that I completely support.

Michael Bublé [Born 1975] Ted Gioia describes Michael Bublé, and lesser-known vocalists *"as channeling Frank Sinatra through Harry Connick, without much Jazz sensitivity."*[256] Gioia then beautifully captures reality. *"With his Rat Pack stage presence that seems to tap into some subliminal desire to resurrect the glamour of days long gone and entertainers dearly departed."*[257]

Lady vocalists

For the last two generations, Canada has produced many excellent lady vocalists. Few of them have created a world-wide following, but each of them has been immensely popular in Canada and are well worth listening to.

The Matriarch of Canada's lady vocalists is Jackie Richardson

Jackie Richardson [Born 1947] is an award-winning actor and one of Canada's foremost singers of gospel, blues, and Jazz whose career includes performances in concert, radio, television, and recordings. She has performed across Canada and in other countries around the world.

The Toronto Star's Commemoration of Toronto's 180th birthday honored Jackie as one of 180 people considered to have helped shape our city. High on Jackie's list of social needs is a passionate desire to bring more focus and support to women and children's issues.

In terms of lasting popularity, Holly Cole and Molly Johnson are difficult to separate, but in terms of style, unique

Holly Cole [Born 1963] has been performing and recording since 1983, some as a soloist, but much of it in a trio with bassist David Piltch and pianist Aaron Davis. Holly is a singer you must listen to. Every recording is so perfectly arranged and performed that you dare not miss a note.

She is praised as an interpretative singer working between the realms of Jazz and pop. Her unique interpretations are applauded as being highly musical, intensely original, sophisticated, witty, and sexy. In her hands, even familiar compositions – from Hank Williams to Cole Porter – enjoy the potential to shine like never before. *Holly never fails to present her music with style, humour, and grace, sending it out on journeys straight to the listener's heart.*[258] Her perfection and consistency are unmatched.

Molly Johnson [Born 1959] is a multiple award-winning singer-songwriter and philanthropist. Discussing her latest recording "Meaning to Tell Ya" gives us a real insight into her talents and versatility' It is more than a Jazz record. It's funk, its soul, it's groove. Producer Larry Klein says: *"Molly has the kind of musical gift that cannot be cultivated by musical education or assiduous practice. She has great natural musical instincts, and an irresistible signature to her voice. She is a rare and wonderful talent.*[259] "

This is one such album, a personal, soulful set of originals and covers sung by one of Canada's finest ladies of song, Molly Johnson.

Johnson sings her life experience into these songs, and the results are riveting, moving and celebratory. As a superb storyteller, Johnson mixes playfulness, memorable melodic hooks, and great grooves, along with many things to ponder.[260] "

As a stage performer, Molly is a true delight. Her great singing is supported by Canada's top Jazz musicians, and the evening is made complete with many anecdotes and a joyous sense of humour. The talented Johnson family includes sister Taborah, a singer and actor.

The next two ladies are my favourite Canadian Jazz Vocalists

Sophia Perlman [Born 1985] is singer, musician, songwriter, arts facilitator, choral conductor, music director and educator. Along with her husband Adrean Farrugia, she is a member of Mohawk College Faculty.

Her musical maturity and impressive ability as an improviser have made her a first call not only by bandleaders but also as a frequent guest of Toronto's top musicians and ensembles including Richard Underhill, Richard Whiteman, The Toronto Jazz Orchestra the late Jeff Healey.

She is also the featured vocalist with The Vipers, whose self-titled, second album was released in November of 2011. I think her period with the Vipers, led by Howard Moore and Pat Carey, was the highpoint of her career

When Sophia and The Vipers had their debut performance in October of 2005 there were those who wondered if the then twenty-year-old vocalist Sophia Perlman would survive the tough-sell Monday night slot. Not only have they survived, but they have received an overwhelming response, drawing veteran Jazz fans[261]

Monday evening at the Reservoir was a good as you can get, with other musicians, as well as Jazz fans filling the club.

Where Sophia differs from other vocalists is that she is part of the band, not a soloist. My favourite track on the Vipers recording is "You're Driving me crazy," a standard from the 1930s.

If you Like Holly Cole, you must listen to **Melissa Stylianou** [Born 1976]. Jazz vocalist, lyricist, and educator, she was praised by piano master Fred Hersch for her *"gorgeous instrument, superb musicianship, and great taste,[262]"* is considered both a gifted songwriter and a bold, imaginative interpreter of wide-ranging material spanning diverse genres.

Most of her recordings are beautifully arranged Jazz standards and that is her real strength. One of my favourite recordings "East of the Sun and West of the Moon."

There are sad stories in Jazz History. This one always moves me. "East of the Sun and West of the Moon" was written by Brooks Bowman, an undergraduate at Princeton University. His promising songwriting career was cut short, he died three years later, in a car crash.

The song has become a Standard and has been recorded by top names in Jazz, including Ella FitzGerald, Sarah Vaughan, Frank Sinatra, Tony Bennett, and Benny Goodman.

Melissa, like so many Canadian Jazz musicians, moved to New York, where there are more opportunities. She is now part of Duchess, a three-part close harmony vocal group, reminiscent of The Andrews Sisters and The Boswell Sister. I wish there were more music like that.

Melissa was a regular performer at the Rex Hotel, Toronto's premier Jazz Club. By coincidence, the day I am writing my profile of her [August 26th, 2023] Melissa has returned home to Toronto, and to her musical alma mater, The Rex Hotel, where she worked as a server for many years while honing her craft.[263]

Canada has produced countless successful lady vocalists. If you live in Canada, you will be familiar with these ladies. If you live outside Canada, you should listen to a few tracks, and see which you want to add to your playlist.

I suggest you listen to Peter Appleyard's album" Sophisticated Ladies," which features many of the best lady vocalists of the period.

You will hear Emilie-Claire Barlow, Jill Barber, Elizabeth Shepherd, Sophie Millman. Carol Weisman, Barbra Lica, and Diana Panton

I would add Alex Pangman and Nikki Yanofski to my list of sophisticated Canadian ladies.

The Greatest Jazz Musician Ever

There are many lists of the so-called Greatest Jazz Musician of all time. Charlie Parker, John Coltrane, Miles Davis, Thelonius Monk, and Charles Mingus dominate those lists. This will surprise no one.

Duke Ellington and Count Basie show up frequently, but because they are primarily bandleaders, rather than musicians, I have excluded them from my voting.

Singers Ella Fitzgerald and Billie Holiday also appear regularly and along with Sarah Vaughan would top my list of Jazz vocalists.

As a proud Canadian, I was pleased to see how often Oscar Peterson appeared in a Top Ten.

I was surprised to see another name, which frequently ranked as high as, or even higher than Davis, Parker, and Coltrane. That name was **Louis Armstrong**, and he got my vote as the greatest Jazz musician of all time.

Louis Armstrong

*"He played trumpet like nobody else,
put it down & sang a song like no one else."[264]*

That was Eddie Condon's view. What makes Louis Armstrong so great? He had enormous talent, but more than that, he was unique. There is no one that you can compare him with. His talent was obvious when he replaced King Oliver in Kid Ory's band. That was just the start.

An article in the Smithsonian Year of Music[265] called him the *"first great Jazz soloist."* The article goes on to say that Armstrong's improvisations permanently altered the landscape of Jazz by making the soloist the focal point of the performance. Armstrong influenced every Jazz musician who appeared after him. "Dizzy" Gillespie, said *"no him, no me,"*[266] explaining that Armstrong was the foundation of his music.

But Armstrong had help in those early days. There is a well-known saying that "behind every great man is a great woman" That woman was Lil Hardin. Lil is generally regarded as the greatest female Jazz Musician ever. She collaborated with Armstrong on numerous recordings throughout the 1920s. *"Hardin even mentored him on how to dress fashionably and manage his money to best effect, so as to navigate the music scene, as well as being the person to convince him to leave King Oliver's band and start his own."*[267]

This led to Armstrong's success as a bandleader and the Hot Five and Hot Seven recordings from 1925 to 1928. Armstrong laid down the basic vocabulary of Jazz improvisation and became its founding and most influential exponent. It was during this period that Armstrong's unique vocals appeared.

Another of Armstrong's guardian angels appeared in the form of Norman Granz in 1956. Granz had the inspirational idea of creating a duo of Armstrong and Ella Fitzgerald. It seems an unlikely partnership, but they both showed their enormous talent by producing three albums. By now we have seen his amazing versatility.

In 1964, the music charts in the USA were dominated by the Beatles. Armstrong reluctantly recorded Hello Dolly, and it immediately topped the Billboard charts. The news was *"Armstrong beats the Beatles."*[268]

His influence outlived him "What a Wonderful World" was an attempt to ease racial tension in the USA, but the president of the ABC, refused to promote the record It was not until the recording was used in the movie "Good Morning Vietnam" in 1988, that it became a worldwide hit. Sadly, Louis Armstrong had died 17 years earlier.

The purity of the sound of Louis Armstrong's playing probably makes him the most readily recognized trumpet player ever. The Hot Five and Hot Seven proved his worth as bandleader.

In duets with Ella Fitzgerald, his amazing vocal talents emerged. The crossover hits of the 1960s showed his versatility, and he also appeared in thirty movies.

A True Renaissance Man.

Exploring Jazz Further

"Music is your own experience, your own thoughts, your wisdom. If you don't live it, it won't come out of your horn.[269]

Charlie Parker

Before I embarked on this adventure, I had listened to a great deal of Jazz, but I don't think I had ever read a book about Jazz. There are many knowledgeable Jazz writers, whose experience and insights helped me greatly in understanding the musicians, and the world of Jazz.

Sadly, very few Jazz books have been published since about 2010. This doesn't cause a real problem when looking at 20th Century Jazz. It does mean that you need to discover many sources when exploring the 21st Century.

The book I referred to most was the "Penguin Jazz Guide." Morton and Cook [Penguin Books 2010] It combines an enormous knowledge of Jazz and an exceptional understanding of each era of music. Sadly, with the death of Richard Cook, the last edition was published in 2010.

One of the most prolific Jazz Writers is Ted Gioia. He is a very entertaining author and the book I enjoyed most was Jazz Standards [Oxford University Press, 2012]. So much Jazz music consists of adaptations of 1930s show music, and his book helps put so many tunes into context.

Another writer I enjoyed was Ben Ratcliff. Jazz Editor for the New York Times. His book "The Jazz Ear" [Times Books, 2008] influenced me in my writing. The concept is simple. He sits down with well-known Jazz musicians, listening to them discussing music they liked. It provided an amazing insight into people I had only heard before.

The best book about the 21st century that I found is "The Ugly Beauty Jazz in the 21st Century" by Phil Freeman [Zero Books 2021] It is not theoretical speculation on what might happen to Jazz. He talks about the young musicians who are making an impact on the Jazz scene. Some I knew and others I found out more about by listening to their music.

There are other books I added to my library simply because I enjoyed them so much. I should perhaps say at this point that I like real books, that you can touch and hold. I don't get that same satisfaction with e-books.

My first choice would be "Jazz Covers" by Joaquim Paulo,[Taschen America LLC 2022] Many of them are true works of art. Blue Note has always stressed the importance of an album's cover. Did you realize just how important a part multi-media played in Jazz.? I am not sure I was.

My next choice would be "Great Jazz Interviews." [Downbeat 75th Anniversary Edition. [Hal Leonard 2009] Most of them are very entertaining, but as much as the words I enjoyed the pictures…. As you browse you ask yourself questions like "Why did everyone think Chet Baker was so good-looking? And "I didn't know Sonny Rawlins was ever young.

"Birdland Jazz Corner of the World," by Leo T Sullivan [Schiffer Publishing, 2018] is a delightful history of Birdland. which contributed so much to the world of Jazz in just sixteen short years. There are excellent biographies of musicians associated with Birdland, including, of course, Charlie "Yardbird" Parker.

Maybe I am still a child at heart, and I love the pictures. Who could resist a picture of Art Tatum and Earl Hines, sitting at a piano together?

My last recommendation is an intriguing mixture of fact and fiction called "Bebop Fairy Tales," by Mark Ruffin [Ruffin Creative Works, 2020]is about real musicians put into real-life situations. There are three stories, my favourite being the one about Gene Ammons. I have no idea how many of the hilarious incidents happened, but it doesn't really matter, Another story features Lee Morgan, somehow caught up in the life of a local baseball team. It is a joyous book to read. Ruffin himself calls it "A historical fiction of Jazz, Intolerance and Baseball."

To add to your reading, make full use of YouTube. It has an amazing selection of Jazz videos. You might also want to explore the free streaming service of Tubi. It was there I got my first real introduction to lady bandleaders during WWII.

There are of course Jazz Magazines, websites, and newsletters. I want to recommend one to you. Jazz Fuel [https://jazzfuel.com/] is written and published by Matt Fripp. It is a great source of information about musicians, music, lists and thought-provoking challenges. Thank you, Matt.

In the last one hundred years, Jazz has created a goldmine of discovery. It is impossible to resist exploring, and now I have just about reached the end of this journey, I must catch up with about 20 CDs I haven't listened to yet. I wonder what I will discover next.

Jazz Greats of the Next Generation

I have one message for young musicians around the world: Stay true to your heart, believe in yourself, and work hard.[270]

Joe Cocker

You will recall from earlier in the book I was sad, but maybe not totally surprised to discover that all but Herbie Hancock from my 10 Greatest Musicians were dead.

That doesn't make them any less great, but they leave a big hole to fill, if Jazz is not to die, as so many pessimists have mournfully predicted. Others must become the next generation of Jazz Greats. I set out to see.

Currently I have a list of fifty young musicians whom I think may be regarded as Greats in 2050. My definition of "young" was being born in or later than 1980. This gave them a good chance of still playing in 2050 at the age of seventy or less.

This arbitrary date led to the exclusion of incredibly talented musicians, including Hiromi, Norah Jones, and Robert Glasper.

Already exciting facts are emerging. There are many instruments, and several nationalities represented, and male and female musicians share my Top 50 spots.

Much of these young musicians' success will depend on their talent, but there are other factors as well. Izzy Garcia is an amazing drummer, and although she is a member of Maqueque, I am not convinced, that being based in Cuba, she will get the exposure to make it right to the top.

Who is going to end up at the top of my list? I am going to spend a lot of time over the next few months listening and learning.

Hopefully, you will accept the challenge of creating your own list.

Epilogue

This has been a wonderful adventure for me. I felt a little guilty at times having totally ignored my former project management disciplines. But no one had defined the scope, no one had set a completion date, and I was the only resource on the project. This gave me so much room to explore anything that caught my interest.

Have my views on Jazz altered as I have written this material? I don't think so. I still listen to Jazz in the same way, as I did all those years when Kid Ory first hooked me on Jazz. What has happened is that it has added to my appreciation of the Jazz I liked. Seeing musicians rather than just hearing them has extended my appreciation and enjoyment of their music. I often reflect on how the seed planted by Kid Ory's Muskrat Ramble has grown into a magnificent tree.

There were moments of sheer joy, like when a retired Oliver Jones and an elderly Oscar Peterson played together for the first time. The respect, the admiration, and I might also say love between them, added a whole new dimension to the music.

Perhaps even more important is the fact that I have had more time to read about them as people and to understand how their upbringing and social environment influenced their music. This facet of learning was perfectly demonstrated by Camille Thurman in her TV story of Bessie Smith's life and music.

My adventure has put Jazz in context and opened new avenues for exploration.

Over the years I have been very conservative and traditional in my choice of Jazz listening. I may never appreciate two of the Jazz greats: Miles Davis and John Coltrane, but the memory of them is secure, and I now understand the contribution they made to the future of Jazz.

One of the outcomes of listening to Miles Davis was a new appreciation of Hard Bop and I now listen to Weather Report repeatedly.

During this time, I also realized that I had totally underestimated the power of the piano. I have added several pianists to my playlist.

It includes Ramsey Lewis, Tyner McCoy, Geri Allen, Eliane Elias, Hiromi, and Mary Lou Williams

Despite the predictions, Jazz has not died. But it constantly needs a transfusion of new blood. I have started to embrace the new, to do my part in keeping Jazz alive and vibrant.

My next project seeks to look into the future of Jazz and predict who the stars of tomorrow will be. I hope when the time comes you will join me in the fun.

Thank you

Tony Carter

May 2024

About the Author

"As a writer, you should not judge, you should understand. [271]
Ernest Hemingway

Tony Carter is a retired College Professor and Project Manager. He moved from England to Canada in 1985 and lives in Toronto. His love of Jazz started when, as a teenager, discovered Kid Ory's "Muskrat Ramble." He then became an avid follower of Traditional Jazz. He was unaware of the wonderful Jazz music that was being created in the USA, partly because American musicians were not allowed to play in the UK.

It was the movies "The Glenn Miller Story" and "The Benny Goodman Story" that triggered him to recognize the Jazz World was much bigger than he. His listening of the following few years stretched from Swing to Big Band to Dave Brubeck and Modern Jazz Quartet.

And so, a "Lifetime of Jazz" was underway. Apart from a few years in the early 1960s, when living in Liverpool, he got caught up in Beatlemania, but then so did half the world, his love of Jazz has continued.

When he moved to Canada, Jazz interest was past its peak, but there was still a lot of good Jazz to listen to and enjoy.

He is currently following some of the young musicians who are emerging, and predicting which of those will become the Jazz Greats of the next generation. These are the people who will keep Jazz alive

It has been a long lifetime, with hopefully many more years to come. Maybe the highlight of this time, watching Les Paul at his Monday night gig at the Iridium will be surpassed.

If you would like to share part of " Your Lifetime of Jazz" Tony can be contacted at tonycarter16@outlook.com.

At the time of publications all links worked. However, websites to get updated and links no longer work. I have found that in most cases you can find the original quote via a Google search.

I encourage you to follow some of these links, particularly where there is a video. It will add a new dimension to my text. I think my favourite must be "The International Sweethearts of Rhythm"

1 The Essential Jazz Recordings. Published McClelland and Stewart 2006

2 https://quotefancy.com/quote/1787716/Chris-Barber-Jazz-of-the-sort-we-play-is-a-happy-extroverted-music-You-don-t-have-to

3 https://www.theguardian.com/music/2011/jul/08/otillie-patterson-blues-singer-obituary

4 www.thepeoplehistory.com/50smusic.html

5 First Time! The Count Meets the Duke

6http://www.plosin.com/beatbegins/projects/boyd.html#:~:text=Kenton's%20sound%20was%20more%20aggressive,techniques%20used%20within%20the%20band.

7https://nationaljazzarchive.org.uk/explore/interviews/1635416-pete-rugolo?

8 https://music.apple.com/td/song/apple-honey/282671317 U

9 https://www.youtube.com/watch?v=1tnI2u8ML4Y

10 Kernfeld, Barry (1999). "Clarke, Kenny". American National Biography. Oxford University Press.

11 https://www.jstor.org/stable/10.1525/jm.2009.26.2.133

12 Dave Brubeck - Wikipedia

13 The Great Jazz Day Art Kane 1999

14 The Great Jazz Day Art Kane 1999

15 The Essential Jazz Recordings by Ross Porter: 9780771070327 | PenguinRandomHouse.com: Books

16 https://jazzonthetube.com/video/presents-improvisation-1950/

17 https://www.apassion4jazz.net/quotations5.html

18 Birdland. The Jazz corner of the world. Leo T. Sullivan. Schiffer Press 2018

19 https://www.azquotes.com/quote/1023838

20 https://www.allgreatquotes.com/quote-361222/

21 Late in 2011, UNESCO designated 30 April as International Jazz Day to highlight Jazz and its diplomatic role of uniting people. International Jazz Day is pioneered by the Director-General of UNESCO and by Herbie Hancock, UNESCO Ambassador for Intercultural Dialogue.

22 The 2017 event was sponsored by the Thelonious Monk Institute of Jazz, which exists to promote common values of tolerance, respect for human rights and social inclusion.

23 Richard Cook [1957-2007] and Brian Morton [Born 1957]. British Jazz journalists

24 Rethinking Jazz through the 70's https://doi.org/10.1080/17494061003694121

25 The Penguin Jazz Guide. Brian Morton and Richard Cook. Penguin Books 2010

26 https://www.npr.org/transcripts/753195250

27 https://minimalistquotes.com/john-lewis-quote-18963/

28 https://wyntonmarsalis.org/news/entry/a-Jazz-success-story-with-a-tinge-of-the-blues- at-lincoln-center

29 https://www.nytimes.com/1998/09/22/arts/high-notes-low-special-report-jazz-success-story-with-tinge-blues-lincoln-center.html

30 Passed by the House of Representatives September 23, 1987, Passed by the Senate December 4, 1987

31 https://Jazztimes.com/features/columns/thirty-years-of-our-Jazztimes-the-1980's

32 https://www.msmnyc.edu/about/history/

33 Penguin Jazz Guide. Morton and Cook. 2010

34 https://Jazztimes.com/features/columns/thirty-years-of-our-Jazztimes-the-1990s/

35 https://www.penguinrandomhouse.ca/books/309043/the-penguin-jazz-guide-by-brian-morton/9780141048314

36 Ken Burns "The History of Jazz. 10-part video series

37 https://rateyourmusic.com/list/Rifugium/Jazz_in_the_21st_century

38 https://rateyourmusic.com/list/Rifugium/Jazz_in_the_21st_century/

39 nkx.org/Jazz/2022-04-29/reflecting-the-time-in-which-its-created-21st-century-modern- Jazz-is-a-rainbow-of-global-cultures.

40 Duke Ellington quote: There are two kinds of music. Good music, and the…

41ttps://www.penguinrandomhouse.ca/books/309043/the-penguin-jazz-guide-by-brian-morton/9780141048314

42 Quoted in https://www.goodreads.com/quotes/575916-where-s-jazz-going-i-don-t-know-maybe-it-s-going-to#:~:text=Sign%20Up%20Now-,Where's%20jazz%20going%3F,t%20make%20anything%20go%20anywhere.o

43 https://songwrightsapothecarylab.com/

44 https://www.bbc.com/news/entertainment-arts-58112962

45 Playing Changes: Jazz for the New Century

46 https://www.allmusic.com/artist/c%C3%A9cile-mclorin-salvant-mn0003003564/biography

47 https://www.classicfm.com/discover-music/latest/quotes-classical-musicians/glenn-gould/

48 Glenn Gould was a renowned Canadian Classical Pianist. I was surprised at just how admired he was by Jazz pianists www.classicfm.com/discover-music/latest/quotes-classical-musicians/glenn-gould/

49 The History of Jazz, 2nd Edition. Published 2011. Oxford University Press

50 http://cioc8-1.weebly.com/scott-joplin.html African Americans Carving their way into US History

51 This is adapted from a biography written by Scott Yanow. https://www.allmusic.com/artist/art- tatum-mn0000505770/biography

52 https://courses.dcs.wisc.edu/wp/musicalperformers/art-tatum/

53 Quoted from https://greggbaker-10616.medium.com/art-tatum-64a768e11dec

54 Gene Ammons, the saxophone player is Albert's son.

55 https://www.amazon.ca/Blues-Robert-Johnson-Cray/dp/0028648862

56 Joseph Vernon "Big Joe" Turner Jr. (1911 –1985) was an American "blues shouter" from Kansas City, Missouri. According to songwriter Doc Pomus, "Rock and roll would have never happened without him"

57https://www.theguardian.com/music/2007/dec/27/Jazz.johnfordham

58 https://www.nytimes.com/2007/12/25/arts/25peterson.html

59 https://www.youtube.com/watch?reload=9&v=YAeT3Dr74Ys

60https://www.historicalsocietyottawa.ca/publications/ottawa-stories/personalities-from-the-very-famous-to-the-lesser-known/the-maharaja-of-the-keyboard. This quote is also attributed to Roy Eldridge

[61] <u>Oscar Peterson, Virtuoso of Jazz, Dies at 82 - The New York Times (nytimes.com)</u>

[62] The Claude Bampton Orchestra was founded and funded but the National Institute for the Blind in 1936 and was made up of twenty musicians, eighteen of who were blind. Conducted by Claude Bampton who used an oversized baton that made sounds to direct the musicians,

[63] His vibraphone players included the great Cal Tjader [1925 – 1982]

[64]https://academic.oup.com/book/39631/chapter-abstract/339587065?redirectedFrom=fulltext&login=false

[65] "On the Road" Jack Kerouac. Published 1951

[66] Original source of quote no longer available

[67] Eldee Young and Ramsey Lewis were schoolmates and worked together for 10 years.

[68] The music they played is available on You Tube, but I have not been able to track the interviews

[70] Quoted from https://www.songfacts.com/facts/herbie-hancock/watermelon-man

[71] https://www.herbiehancock.com/biography-full-page/

[72]https://www.theguardian.com/music/musicblog/2010/oct/13/miles-davis-second-great-quintet

[73]<u>https://www.herbiehancock.com/biography-full-page/</u>

[74] https://www.herbiehancock.com/

[75] Hank was the oldest. His younger brother was cornetist band leader, composer, and arranger Thad Jones. The baby of the family, drummer Elvin Jones, was a major force behind John Coltrane's quartet.

[76] "The Jazz Ear". Ben Ratcliff. Times Books 2008

[77] https://www.azquotes.com/author/21186-Mary_Lou_Williams

[78] https://www.npr.org/2019/09/10/749743012/how-mary-lou-williams-shaped-the-sound-of-the-big-band-era

[79] <u>Marian McPartland obituary | Jazz | The Guardian</u>

[80] https://www.alicecoltrane.com/

[81] https://sheshreds.com/brandee-younger/

[82] The notes before this point are adapted from the New York Times obituary. https://www.nytimes.com/2017/06/27/arts/music/geri-allen-dead-Jazz.html

[83] Much of the material above is taken from Renee Rosnes website

[84] Reneerosnes.com/biography

[85] https://reneerosnes.com/

[86] http://elianeelias.com/bio/

[87]https://elianeelias.com/bio/#:~:text=In%20review%20of%20Elias'%20unique,with%20life%20and%20natural%20beauty%E2%80%9D

[88] https://elianeelias.com/bio/

[89] https://www.hiromi-home.com/

[90] Stanley Clark [Born 1951] is one of the few Jazz musicians who played both electric and upright bass. His breakthrough came an album he made with Chick Corea in 1970 called "Return to Forever."

[91] Drummer Lennie White has been described as "one of the fathers of Jazz Fusion and was also featured on Return to Forever."

[92] https://sandymusiclab.com/guitar-quotes/

[93] The Charlie Christian Collection 1939-1941 Acrobat Music 2013

[94] Simon, George T. (1971). The Big Bands. ISBN 0-02-872430-5.

[95] Martin Taylor [Born 1956] is a British Jazz guitar player. He was strongly influenced by Django Reinhardt and played with Stephane Grappelli for 11 years.

[96] There is a recording the brothers made with George Shearing

[97] https://www.encyclopedia.com/people/literature-and-arts/music-popular-and-Jazz- biographies/john-leslie-montgomery

[98] Guitar Players: One Instrument and Its Masters in America. James Sallis. Publ. 1982. William Morrow

[99] https://www.youtube.com/watch?v=VBGZgyl72_g

[100] https://www.pop-music.ca/milt-jackson-wes-montgomery-bags-meets-wes-vinyl.html

[101] Quoted from https://Jazzresearch.com/Jazz-scene-usa-12-barney-kessel/

[102] Nesuhi Ertegun was a Turkish-American Record Producer

[103] Quoted in https://www.biography.com/musician/les-paul

[104] https://www.guitarworld.com/artists/top-10-les-paul-moments

105 These notes are an edited version of Ed Bickert's obituary in Jazz Times https://Jazztimes.com/features/tributes-and-obituaries/guitarist-ed-bickert-dies-at-86/

106 https://www.youtube.com/watch?reload=9&v=teXOPAFMOp0

107 New York Media, LLC (17 September 1979). New York Magazine. New York Media, LLC

108 Evelyn Glennie was a Scottish percussionist. She was deaf from the age of eight Evelyn heard music by sensing the notes in different parts of her body.

109 Art Tatum With Lionel Hampton, Buddy Rich – The Tatum / Hampton / Rich Trio. Recorded 1955

110 https://playback.fm/charts/top-100-songs/video/1942/The-Ink-Spots-Every-Night-About-This- Time

111 TOP 12 QUOTES BY LIONEL HAMPTON | A-Z Quotes (azquotes.com)

112 https://www.allmusic.com/artist/milt-jackson-mn0000489845/biography

113 https://concord.com/concord-albums/gary-burton-for-hamp-red-bags-and-cal/

114 Yogi Berra Explains Jazz | David J. Elliott (davidelliottmusic.com)

115 The Jazz Ear. Ben Ratcliff. Published Henry Holt Inc. 2008

116 Quoted from The Jazz Ear. Ben Ratcliff

117 https://www.brainyquote.com/authors/humphrey-lyttelton-quotes

118 Dan Morgenstern, Editor of Metronome Magazine [Reprinted in A Great Day in Jazz

119https://www.allaboutJazz.com/buddy-bolden-the-insane-life-of-the-founder-father-of- Jazz-buddy-bolden-by-jeff-winke.php?width=1280

120 https://boldenmovie.com/#home

121 https://read-the-plaque.appspot.com/plaque/charles-joseph-buddy-bolden

122 The Essential Jazz Recordings. Ross Porter. 2006. Publ. McClelland and Stewart

123 Quotes in The Penguin Jazz Guide, Page 21

124 https://waldina.com/2020/08/04/happy-119th-birthday-louis-armstrong/

125 http://www.Jazzquotations.com/search/label/Ella%20Fitzgerald%20Quotes

126 https://www.quotemaster.org/q64b9d0eb9c9aad599215fc913669a787

127https://www.independent.co.uk/arts-entertainment/obituary-harry-edison-1109279.html

128 Quoted in https://www.biography.com/musician/dizzy-gillespie

129 Quoted in https://Jazzfuel.com/best-Jazz-trumpet-players/#Dizzy_Gillespie

130 https://www.last.fm/music/Miles+Davis/+wiki

131 http://www.Jazzquotations.com/search/label/Miles%20Davis

132 Quoted in an obituary
https://www.nydailynews.com/entertainment/music/miles-davis- Jazz-pioneer-dies-65-1991-article1.2376885https://www.nydailynews.com/entertainment/music/miles-davis- Jazz-pioneer-dies-65-1991-article-1.2376885

133 https://quotefancy.com/quote

134 Quoted from https://drownedinsound.com/releases/20164/reviews/4151533

135 https://andscape.com/features/for-wynton-marsalis-forgetting-the-roots-of-jazz-is-forgetting-the-history-of-race-in-america/

136 Link has been deleted

137 https://libquotes.com/miles-davis/quote/lbk3d9g

138 https://www.quoteslyfe.com/quote/Well-if-I-could-play-like-Wynton-463588

139 https://www.quoteslyfe.com/quote/Well-if-I-could-play-like-Wynton-463588

140 https://genius.com/Miriam-makeba-soweto-blues-lyrics

141https://www.kcrw.com/culture/shows/lost-notes/hugh-masekela-miriam-makeba

142 https://www.kcrw.com/culture/shows/lost-notes

143 Jack Teagarden: Steady rockin' with Satchmo (nepm.org)

144 https://study.com/academy/lesson/trombone-history-parts-facts.html

145 The notes on the evolution of the Trombone in Jazz is based on
https://www.allaboutJazz.com/trombone-by-bob-bernotas.php

146 Much of the material on Kid Ory is based on his NY Times Obituary
https://www.nytimes.com/1973/01/24/archives/kid-ory-86-dead-Jazz-trombonist-exponent-of-dixieland-slide-wrote.html

147https://riverwalkJazz.stanford.edu/program/tailgate-swing-history-Jazz-trombone

[148]https://music.allpurposeguru.com/2015/08/kid-ory-trombonist-businessman/

[149] Much of the material in the J.J. Johnson section are adapted from the Scott Yanow biography in AllMusic.

[150] TOP 16 QUOTES BY PAUL DESMOND | A-Z Quotes (azquotes.com)

[151] https://en.wikipedia.org/wiki/Saxophone

[152]https://www.udiscovermusic.com/artist/charlie-parker//

[153]https://www.udiscovermusic.com/stories/charlie-parker-Jazz-history/

[154] https://www.azquotes.com/quote/1269601

[155]https://www.udiscovermusic.com/stories/charlie-parker-Jazz-history/#:~:text=Not%20that%20everyone%20%E2%80%9Cgot%E2%80%9D%20what,re calls%20how%20conscientious%20they%20were

[156]https://www.udiscovermusic.com/stories/charlie-parker-Jazz-history/#:~:text=In%201943%2C%20Parker%20played%20in,began%20playing%20the%20tenor%20sax.

[157] Story told in "The Essential Jazz Recordings" by Ross Porter

[158] Watch Jazz | A Documentary Film by Ken Burns | PBS

[159]https://www.allmusic.com/album/a-love-supreme-w0000187827

[160] Quoted in Ross Porter's The Essential Jazz Recordings

[161] https://www.notablebiographies.com/supp/Supplement-Fl-Ka/Getz-Stan.html

[162] https://www.notablebiographies.com/supp/Supplement-Fl-Ka/Getz-Stan.html

[163] Quoted in The New York Times Essential Library. Ben Ratliff

[164] https://www.last.fm/music/Paul+Desmond/+wiki

[165] Quoted in https://www.azquotes.com/quote/534090

[166] This story appears on the Art Blakey website http://artblakey.com/biography/

[167] https://www.allmusic.com/artist/art-blakey-mn0000928942/biography

[168]https://www.udiscovermusic.com/stories/art-blakey-jazz-messenger-hard-bop-drummer/

[169]https://www.theJazzpianosite.com/Jazz-piano-lessons/Jazz-genres/hard-bop-soul-Jazz- explained/

[170] https://www.gkrp.net/biographies/gene-krupa/

[171] https://www.gkrp.net/biographies/gene-krupa/

[172]https://www.encyclopedia.com/education/news-wires-white-papers-and-books/krupa- gene

[173] https://www.veryimportantpotheads.com/krupa.html

[174] http://www.browsebiography.com/bio-gene_krupa.html

[175] https://www.drummerworld.com/drummers/Buddy_Rich.html

[176] https://Jazz-drummer.blogspot.com/2009/08/legend-of-buddy-rich.html

[177] Quoted in https://www.drummerworld.com/drummers/Buddy_Rich.html

[178] https://www.youtube.com/watch?v=WBOohuZlAiM

[179] http://accounts.fyicomminc.com/Jazzmen/roach.htm

[180] http://accounts.fyicomminc.com/Jazzmen/roach.htm

[181] https://www.azquotes.com/quote/1023838

[182] https://www.apassion4jazz.net/quotations2.html

[183] The introductory notes are adapted from Wikipedia https://en.wikipedia.org/wiki/Terri_Lyne_Carrington

[184] https://Jazztimes.com/features/profiles/social-science-becomes-social-art-for-terri-lyne-carringtons-

[185] https://theculturetrip.com/north-america/usa/massachusetts/articles/interview-with-terri-lyne-carrington-i-try-to-paint-as-i-play/

[186]https://theculturetrip.com/northmerica/usa/massachusetts/articles/interview-with-terri-lyne-carrington-i-try-to-paint-as-i-play

[187] https://www.studybass.com/lessons/basics/the-role-of-the-bass/

[188] https://www.discogs.com/release/5549806-Oscar-Peterson-Trio-With-Ray-Brown-Ed- Thigpen-1959

[189] https://legacy.npr.org/programs/Jazzprofiles/archive/brown_ray.html

[190] The Penguin Guide to Jazz

[191] https://www.apassion4jazz.net/quotations5.html

[192] https://tomekareid.com/

[193] https://insheepsclothinghifi.com/10-roland-kirk-live-performances/

[194] https://insheepsclothinghifi.com/10-roland-kirk-live-performances/

[195] https://www.udiscovermusic.com/stories/rahsaan-roland-kirk-the-ed-sullivan-show-feature/ How Rahsaan Roland Kirk Shook Up The Ed Sullivan Show

[196] "Kirk died from a stroke in December 1977 at the age of forty-two,

Kirk reflected on his time with J&MP. "I knew it was something that couldn't last," he explained, "but it was something to show that the musician … does more than put needles in his arm or smoke pot

[197] https://entertainment.ha.com/itm/music-memorabilia/posters/blanche-calloway-1933- sepia-siren-of-syncopation-large-concert-poster/a/7241-90119.s

[198] .https://en.wikipedia.org/wiki/International_Sweethearts_of_Rhythm

[199] https://www.youtube.com/watch?v=WczP3PyHt20

[200] Information for the last two paragraphs is taken from https://www.royalalberthall.com/about-the-hall/news/2021/march/original-girl-power-ivy- benson-and-her-all-girls band/#:~:text=By%20eight%2C%20Ivy%20was%20performing,clarinet%20and%20tr omb one%20as%20well.

[201] https://live.stanford.edu/calendar/march-2022/maria-schneider-orchestra

[202] https://live.stanford.edu/calendar/march-2022/maria-schneider-orchestra

[203] https://sherriemaricle.com/

[204] https://www.youtube.com/watch?v=qFRVoZrwuwo

[205] https://riverwalkjazz.stanford.edu/program/not-just-another-pretty-face-girl-singers- swing- 20her%20career.

[206] https://legacy.apollotheater.org › uploads › 2020/05

[207] Adapted from History https://www.history.com/this-day-in-history/ella-fitzgerald-wins- amateur-night-at-harlems-apollo-theater

[208] https://www.ellafitzgerald.com/biography/#/

[209]https://www.npr.org/sections/ablogsupreme/2011/10/20/141419438/norman-granz- five-recordings-by-the-man-who-used-jazz-for-justice#:~:text=Norman%20Granz%20was%20one%20of,in%20the%20history%20of%20j azz.

[210] wwashttp://www.ellafitzgerald.com/about/biography

[211] Quoted in NY Times Obituary https://www.nytimes.com/1990/04/05/obituaries/sarah- vaughan-divine-one-of-

Jazz-singing-is-dead-at-66.htm

[212] https://www.biography.com/musicians/sarah-vaughan

[213] https://www.biography.com/news/billie-holiday-facts

[214] https://www.udiscovermusic.com/artist/dinah-washington/

[215] https://www.biography.com/musicians/nina-simone

[216] Nina Simone sings the Blues" RCA Records 1967

[217] https://www.nytimes.com/1998/09/01/arts/Jazz-review-a-diva-s-day-rich-with-love- prayer-and-politics.html

[218]https://www.instagram.com/continuum.sd/reel/CL7Bl8RDtvD

[219] https://www.arts.gov/honors/jazz/abbey-lincoln

[220] https://www.arts.gov/honors/Jazz/abbey-lincoln

[221] The political activism of Lincoln and Roach is discussed in the Section on the 1960s

[222] Abbey Lincoln
https://www.youtube.com/watch?reload=9&time_continue=206&v=IF6q6XKKrik &feature=e mb_logo

[223] https://www.udiscovermusic.com/artist/billie-holiday/

[224] https://www.udiscovermusic.com/in-depth-features/blue-note-finest-jazz-since-1939/

[225] https://www.udiscovermusic.com/stories/rediscover-come-away-with-me/

[226] President and CEO of Blue Note

[227] https://www.udiscovermusic.com/stories/rediscover-come-away-with-me/

[228]https://libguides.wustl.edu/c.php?g=853438&p=6110024#:~:text=She%20sang%20about%20the%20kind,be%20hard%2Dpressed%20to%20describe.&text=Hall%20of%20Fame-
,the%20empress%20of%20the%20blues,was%20definitive%2c%20unprecedent ed%20and%20glorious.

[229] https://www.npr.org/2019/09/05/757840971/ella-fitzgeralds-signature-singing-style- explained-by-Jazzmeia-horn

[230] https://www.youtube.com/watch?v=GTl5vKJWhpE

[231] Ma Rainey's Black Bottom. Netflixs 2020

[232] https://www.telegraph.co.uk/news/obituaries/1556510/George-Melly.html 7

[233]https://www.telegraph.co.uk/news/obituaries/1556510/George Melly.html#:~:text=George%20Melly%2C%20the%20Jazz%20singer,the%20public %20for%20five%20decades

[234] Quoted in The Penguin Guide to Jazz, by Brian Morton

[235] https://Jazzfuel.com/best-male-Jazz-singers/

[236] https://www.facebook.com/reel/340639578513449

[237] A guide to understanding how jazz influenced art and culture - Mtltimes.ca

[238] https://www.theJazzresource.com/top_25_Jazz_albums.html

[239] https://ottawacitizen.com/entertainment/jazzblog/rip-ed-bickert

[240] https://www.npr.org/sections/ablogsupreme/2012/07/12/156678757/back-home- with-canadas-greatest-living-Jazz-musician

[241]https://www.youtube.com/watch?v=tvS4Mm_bVEY&list=RDtvS4Mm_bVEY&in dex=1

[242] Note the tribute to Art Blakey and the Jazz Messengers

[243] https://www.soultonecymbals.com/artist/norman-marshall-villeneuve

[244] https://www.opJazzfest.org/dave-young

[245] https://www.theglobeandmail.com/arts/music/mr-swing-archie-alleyne-was-a-mentor-to-young-black-musicians/article25125482/

251

[247]https://www.theglobeandmail.com/arts/music/mr-swing-archie-alleyne-was-a-mentor-to-young-black-musicians/article25125482

[248] https://www.thecanadianencyclopedia.ca/en/article/georges-Jazz-room-emc

[249] https://www.thecanadianencyclopedia.ca/en/article/moe-koffman-emc

[250] https://www.cshf.ca/song/swinging-shepherd-blues; https://www.cshf.ca/song/swinging-shepherd-blues;

[251] https://www.youtube.com/watch?v=odI81Se2UFw

[252]https://stewarthoffmanmusic.com/Jazz-maestro/#:~:text=%E2%80%9CI%20hear%20a%20musical%20sound,on%20it%20 is%20 a%20miracle.%E2%80%9D

[253]https://www.theglobeandmail.com/arts/music/peter-appleyard-one-of-the-giants-of- Jazz/article14174033/

[254] https://tma149.ca/doug-riley-1945-2007-2020-lifetime-achievement-award/

[255] https://robibotos.com/

[256] Ted Gioia The History of Jazz Page 375

[257] Ted Gioia The History of Jazz Page 375

[258] http://www.hollycole.com/about/

[259] https://www.thatericalper.com/2018/05/16/molly-johnsons-new-album-meaning-to-tell-ya-is-out-now/

[260] https://www.thewholenote.com/index.php/booksrecords2/jazzaimprovised/28592- meaning-to-tell-ya-molly-johnson

[261] https://www.clubcrawlers.com/toronto/event/the-vipers

[262] https://www.allaboutjazz.com/musicians/melissa-stylianou

[263] https://www.thestar.com/entertainment/music/down-at-toronto-s-rex-hotel-live-jazz-weaves-its-spell-nightly/article_aadf8d56-d0e7-52ca-a526-a80ac462100.html#:~:text=%E2%80%9CMelissa%20returns%20home%20to%20Toront o,son%2C%

[264] https://www.azquotes.com/author/21091-Eddie_Condon

[265] https://music.si.edu/story/louis-armstrong

[266] https://www.Jazziz.com/free/genius-louis-armstrong/

[267] https://www.prestomusic.com/Jazz/articles/3554--classic-album-review-louis-armstrong-hot-five-and-hot-seven-sessions

[268] https://www.history.com/this-day-in-history/an-unlikely-challenger-ends-the-beatles-reign-atop-the-u-s-pop-charts

[269] https://www.oxfordreference.com/display/10.1093/acref/9780191843730.001.0001/q-oro-ed5-00008142

[270] https://www.brainyquote.com/quotes/joe_cocker_690238

[271] Hemingway's Advice on Writing, Ambition, the Art of Revision, and His Reading List of Essential Books for Aspiring Writers – The Marginalian

www.ingramcontent.com/pod-product-compliance
Lightning Source LLC
Chambersburg PA
CBHW051523120626
46551CB00012B/1049